# Games wit········ ·······s

## Joe Kennedy

Published by Repeater Books
An imprint of Watkins Media Ltd

19-21 Cecil Court
London
WC2N 4EZ
UK

www.repeaterbooks.com
A Repeater Books paperback original 2016
1

Distributed in the United States by Random House, Inc., New York.

Cover design: Johnny Bull
Typography and typesetting: Jan Middendorp
Typefaces: Chaparral Pro and Supria Sans

ISBN: 978-1-910924-24-2
Ebook ISBN: 978-1-910924-25-9

# CONTENTS

# Introduction

There is an anecdote told widely within British football culture which I believe is true when applied to one individual, and suspect is apocryphal in its many other applications. As far as I know, the verified example attaches itself to Len Shackleton, who played for Bradford Park Avenue, Newcastle and, most famously, for Sunderland in the English game's post-World War II Golden Age. In Shackleton's 1956 autobiography, *The Clown Prince of Soccer*, apparently, there is a chapter with the perhaps deliberately un-wieldy title 'The Average Director's Knowledge of Football'. The rest of the page, or the following page, depending on who's telling the story, is completely blank.

I've no desire to explain the joke, largely because it shouldn't require explaining, but is it at all possible that Shackleton was, consciously or unconsciously, making a point other than the obvious one here? Isn't there another way of interpreting what seems to be a throwaway literary sight-gag? Given the story of how football clubs have been owned, and what football's owners have done with clubs, since the halcyon days of Shackleton, Jackie Milburn, Stanley Matthews and Tom Finney, isn't it apparent that what the "average director" – and what a quaint, sepia-tinted term "director" now seems – *really* knows about football is that it, thrillingly and worryingly, lacks intrinsic meaning? By this, I mean that football means nothing whatsoever in its own right, which of course makes it into the ideal vehicle for any number of superimposed meanings.

This is certainly the case not least for those owners and "direc-tors" who have, over the decades, seen football clubs as: instruments of civic and commercial leverage, concentrations of material stuff awaiting asset-stripping, objects of juvenile fantasy, sources of wealth from television and merchandise, and – most notably in the last ten years – political launderettes. Football means something very different for a Middle Eastern petrogarch buying a Premier League side and a South London property developer who purchases a non-league club in order to realise his vision of a Sainsbury's on the site of their ground. That said, in neither case does the game as such really enter the equation.

This is, however, only one part of a far broader antagonism between the game described by the rules and the almost infinitely variable financial, emotional and political investments that are made in its name. From the very first time that you walk into a football ground, you are aware of the way in which the match is at best a single component of, and in some cases utterly periph-eral to, the thing we unreflectively call "football". Speaking as a fan and a (not sensationally good) player of almost three decades' experience, what strikes me now is how central football has been not only to my understanding of more or less obviously related fields such as politics, history and economics, but also of are-as which seem logically separate: literature, music, philosophy, critical theory. As a literature undergraduate at the then still theory-heavy University of East Anglia, my response to an essay task requiring a study of Roland Barthes' ideas about narrative analysis was to illustrate these in relation to the 1970 World Cup final. It was fair payback: the reason literature, particularly of the demonstratively experimental sort, was my subject was at least in part to do with my introduction to various culty authors (Bur-roughs, Kafka, Ballard, Kerouac, Beckett) via football fanzines in the mid-1990s. I was completely unsurprised later on to find out how many theorists – amongst them Jacques Derrida, Umberto Eco and Antonio Negri – were football fans.

That said, I never expected to write a book about football: while I was completing my PhD on wartime British modernism I played as many as three times a week and attended matches reasonably regularly, but predominantly in the name of relieving tension and boredom. It wasn't until a couple of years later, lacking an academic post and living brokely in Boris Johnson's ever-more homogenously bourgeois London that I started to think with any degree of rigour about how football locked into contemporary political formations, and whether or not it could be a site of resistance to neoliberal dominance in spite of the clear influence of neoliberalism at various levels of the game. Nevertheless, I found all too often that I was spending the time in which I could have been putting these ideas to paper going to football and becoming increasingly involved in supporter activism. Naturally, this meant a constant series of fluctuations and modulations in what I thought (or what I thought I thought) about the game. The biggest of these, I believe, was a progression from regarding football, or some football, as the site of a dubiously defined politics of authenticity to a position in which it became an arena in which "authenticity" became subject to conceptual collapse.

As a result, the approach I took to writing this book bifurcated between essays attempting a theoretical, albeit hopefully not grindingly academic, intervention into football and football culture, and accounts of particular matches that prompted some of the shifts in thinking I mention above. Inevitably, this leads to a certain unevenness of tone, although I'd argue in my defence that football itself is tonally inconsistent, given that it is the sum of all the instances in which a remarkably simple sport encounters its non-sporting outside. Derrida, who fantasised about becoming a professional footballer while a child in French Algeria, was surely being flippant or provocative when he claimed "beyond the touchline, there is nothing". Football looks like twenty-two people kicking a ball about on a small patch of grass, or plastic, but it is absolutely not only, and not even mainly, this.

What I've attempted here, then, is a study of what "football" *implies* at a particular moment in (predominantly) British history. There are four travelogues, arranged in chronological order so as to be roughly contemporary with the theoretical development of the four essays, which can be described as follows. The first looks at the time-sense of football, noting that our experience, and perhaps our enjoyment, of the game is melancholy, arranged around a sense of loss. This is contextualised through a reading of early football's historical simultaneity with the development of modernist aesthetics: both, I argue, trace the dematerialising, "melting" effects of industrial capitalism noted by Marx and Engels in a famous passage in *The Communist Manifesto*. Closing the circle, I then look at works of literature which have used football as a structural metaphor for a modernist or avant-garde poetics. Football, I claim here, should be considered a form of popular modernism, potentially possessive of all the radical cachet that implies. My second essay considers the ideological position occupied by football players in the early 21st century, regarding this in the light of contemporary militarism and popular discourses of "passion" and "commitment". I then proceed to look at the gap which yawns between these discourses and the lived reality of being a footballer, particularly for the majority of players who constitute a reserve army of precarious labour mirroring that to be found in neoliberal "society" at large.

In the third essay, I begin by thinking about the attempts to eliminate error from football in the form of goal-line technology and video refereeing. This proceeds into a discussion of the sport's increasingly sophisticated representation in video games, and how such games attempt to simulate the contingencies which simultaneously attract us to football and draw our attention to the *necessary incompletion* of its rules. I then look at how recent forms of tactical and statistical analysis constitute new attempts to reduce football's contingency, thus enabling the final enclosure and commodification of the sport. The final essay examines the centrality of ideas about authenticity to football culture, examining the ways in which such ideas constitute an attempt to organise and limit the politics of footballing meaning. This is ultimately developed into a comparative discussion of the problems faced by a football culture obsessed with authenticity and the struggles of left-wing politics in Britain in 2015.

While this is a book meant to be enjoyed by football fans, I don't believe that it is *essentially* about football, in as much as I don't think football is essentially about football either. Some of what's here counts as literary criticism; there are attempted glosses on various ideas from theorists including Walter Benjamin, Jacques Lacan and Jacques Rancière. Hopefully, these are executed with a touch sufficiently light to prevent what I'm doing from falling into a conceptual niche, but with enough seriousness to avoid flippancy. I wrote this neither predominantly as a football fan nor as a theorist: instead, I wanted to see how the two ideas, football and theory, worked on one another. With this in mind, two lines of critique, both of which amount to essentially the same thing, can be anticipated. The first criticism – in the spirit of full disclosure, this is one which has already been made by football-fan friends in response to earlier articles – is that I'm being over-elaborate about an essentially simple subject. My response to that would be to say that *so much* has been written about football already, and that *so much* still clearly goes unsaid, that it's worth risking allegations of pretension to try and figure out what earlier commentators have missed. The second criticism, I suspect, is more likely to come from the other direction: that all of this is simply an appropriation of a theoretical vocabulary to intellectually decorate a subject I have an unqualifiable personal interest in. To that, I'd have to ask what theories are for, if they can't be used to unpack – and politicise – personal taste.

On the latter note, some of the writing here is more autobiographical than I predicted when first conceived of this book, and I've met (literally) hundreds of people who've given me pause for thought here. Hardly any of them are mentioned by name, but they became the implied readership of this book, and I've had plenty of imaginary conversations with them in which I face down various criticisms of the kind I speculate on above. If you're one of these people, rest assured I've tried my hardest to take on board your own personal spec about "what football is", and I'm very grateful for the debates and arguments on the subject which I hope (and expect) will carry on in real life.

# Barrow 3 – Darlington 0

## 7 JANUARY 2012

Britain's literary culture often asks us to imagine that things – love, trust, life itself – come to an end where the land does. Graham Greene told us as much in *Brighton Rock*; more recently, tawdry, salt-sprayed Margate epitomised coastal closure in Graham Swift's novel *Last Orders*. It is hard to determine whether or not this is a case of poetic fallacy: for all of the seaside's metaphorical potency, there's some anthropological truth in the idea as well, as demonstrated by the clustering retirement homes of Eastbourne and Hunstanton, of Scarborough and Weston-Super-Mare. Those places have been chosen consciously as appropriate settings for personal denouements, in which the sharp air and long horizons permit settlements to be reached with the past.

The stretch of the littoral to which I was headed, as my brother and I pulled into an empty cinema car-park just outside Wolverhampton, was Barrow-in-Furness. Less a tastefully dilapidated Victorian resort than a struggling leftover of marine industry, Barrow's reputation is for bleak vistas and connotations. In a geographical no-man's-land between the Irish Sea and the southern Lake District, the town has been where Britain's nuclear submarines have been manufactured since the Sixties. However, Vickers, the local shipyard, has seen a steady decline in contracts since the end of the Cold War, leading to unemployment and its attendant social effects. People I knew who had visited tended to divorce Barrow from the rest of Cumbria. Like Workington and Whitehaven further up the coast, it was regarded as inassimilable to the county's self-image of nature-loving poets, anthropomorphic animals and heroically-doomed water-speed champions, an intrusion from an austere neighbouring North of factory chimneys, pit-wheels, pigeon racing and union banners. Even after the alleged modernisation of much of neighbouring Lancashire, Yorkshire and Country Durham by call centres and coffee chains, it supposedly exhibited this character.

I was travelling to Barrow in expectation of participating in a finale. This endgame was caught inextricably in the contradictory and often, at least to the outsider, unfathomable changes undergone by the North's socio-economic landscape over the last three decades. For many years, Darlington Football Club typified the cash-poor, character-rich small teams from the coalfields, fishing ports and cotton towns who made up the numbers in the Football League. Like their counterparts in obscurity, they were administrated and financed by a combination of local worthies and self-made men, their boardroom a meeting place of dubiously motivated philanthropy and alderman politicking. Most seasons were a struggle: even when the rates were paid and the taxman appeased, success on the field was rare. They played at Feethams, a riverside ground celebrated for its quaintness, with a wood-framed paddock and a shallow concrete bank which backed onto a 19th-century park laid out by the local Quakers, from whom the club take their nickname.

The tightness of their circumstances meant that every triumph, however inconsequential nationally, was relished. There was a fourth-round FA Cup victory over Chelsea in the 1950s, promotions in the late Sixties and mid-Eighties, and a back-to-back elevation at the beginning of the Nineties. The problems escalated here. With Feethams crumbling, a consignment of steel was purchased from Stockton Racecourse, where a stand was being dismantled, with a view to putting a much-needed roof over the terracing in preparation for the highly anticipated return to the Third Division. Stories conflict about what happened next – the metal may have been lost – but the roof never appeared. It was a bad omen, compounded soon enough by the club's ambitious manager's departure for Leicester City. An aging squad faltered in the higher league, despite costly attempts to buy a way out of trouble. Back in the basement division, a succession of managers laboured in the shadow of directorial infighting, signing veteran stars in fruitless efforts to galvanise an eddying side.

Around them, football in the North East was transforming in a way which reflected a more general confidence exhibited by the region as it started to shake off the traumas of Thatcherism. Forty miles up the A1 motorway, Newcastle United had weathered a disastrous five-year spell to flourish under Kevin Keegan's management. Funded by the Geordie property developer John Hall, they launched a spirited quest to bring national and European success to Tyneside, an area which was in the process of casting off its *Likely Lads* image to reinvent itself as a swaggering regional capital, a Barcelona designed by John Poulson rather than Gaudi. Still closer to home, Middlesbrough built a new stadium with the backing of Teesside haulage magnate Steve Gibson, who also spent large sums to bring international talent to the club he'd supported as a boy. Sunderland, too, found a new home and returned to the top flight. Increasingly, the people of Darlington began to be drawn a little further afield to watch football, with the local club an unattractive contender in the North-Eastern sporting marketplace.

In 1999, a figure arrived who promised to change that. George Reynolds, a one-time Barnados boy, reformed safecracker, and among the UK's wealthiest people thanks to his cornering of the chipboard and work-surface industry, bought the club and promised to take them to the Premier League, building a new stadium on the way. Unused to messiahs, or at least not particularly discerning on the rare occasions they turned up, Darlington's supporters backed Reynolds, who initially seemed determined to keep his word as he lavished money on players. Swiftly, however, he became convinced that a winning team could be assembled for a fraction of the outlay he was making, leading to an abrupt downsizing following a narrow failure to gain promotion. A mixture of youngsters and obscurities therefore played out the last seasons at Feethams, failing to make headway in the league as construction progressed on the new ground. Worse than this was the dawning realisation that the Reynolds Arena, as it was to be known, was embarrassingly disproportionate to the modest requirements of the fanbase. As Darlington moved into the Arena, a state of open warfare existed between the owner and the majority of the supporters. The stadium, an ice-cold bowl of empty seats and echoing concourses, became off-limits to his critics. Most notoriously, a teenage fanzine editor, laughably compared to Goebbels by Reynolds, was banned from the ground; other opponents were allegedly subject to menacing late-night phone calls.

By the time the club shrugged off their hubristic owner, they were in administration and, yet again, fighting to remain in the league. Spirited performances saved them on the field, however, and new owners cut costs and spent prudently to assemble a reasonable, if inconsistent, side. Even as the football improved, however, gates dwindled. A new owner, George Houghton, covered the shortfall with his own money, but pulled out in 2009 leaving behind one of the highest wage bills at the level and instigating a second spell in administration. A collapse into the purgatory of non-league ensued, and, although incoming owner Raj Singh backed a triumph at Wembley in the FA Trophy (a knockout competition contested predominantly by semi-professional clubs) in 2011, it was clear that another crisis loomed. Just how quickly this occurred stunned supporters, who had hoped vainly that the Trophy might be a launchpad for reconstruction: in November 2011, following a predictably unsuccessful attempt to renegotiate the players' wages, Singh left.

It looked terminal this time. The ground, encumbered with covenants forbidding non-sporting use, was in the hands of the previous administrators, who loaned it to the club for a nominal sum. Darlington's only income streams were meagre ticket sales, occasional player transfers, and the pin-money of match-day income from programmes, food and drink. Accordingly, many of the non-playing staff were axed; the youth-team manager Craig Liddle, a well-regarded centre-half in the Reynolds-era team, took over management as senior players responded to the club's defaulting on their salaries by leaving. Bringing a number of his protégés into the fray, Liddle oversaw the club as they scraped through their Christmas fixtures. The media, however, became convinced that the short trip to West Cumbria would be Darlington's last journey, and contingency plans were made for a so-called "phoenix" side who would start playing at local league level in August 2012. With this in mind, the visit to Barrow was being presented as a wake. Lapsed supporters talked of returning from abroad to attend.

I vacillated as the day approached. I'd been attending since 1990, but the club's departure from Feethams, and my own moves to East Anglia, Central Europe and eventually South London had left me relatively ambivalent. When I had cash, I'd attend flurries of games, preferring away matches at clubs with grounds less faceless than our Arena; when I was broke, I'd check the score online or text my brother. I wrote on the fans' message board, but my contributions were almost exclusively nostalgic posts about the 1990s. When I played seven-a-side, I wore a Darlington shirt, but it was fourteen years old. Being a part-time follower of a North-Eastern also-ran seemed worthier than dabbling with Chelsea or Liverpool, but I felt a dilettante all the same.

Yet Barrow seemed a brilliantly poetic place for an ending, and my awkwardness about being involved began to be displaced by a familiar, prickly excitement. My brother told me that, if I could reach Wolverhampton, he'd arranged a space for me in a car going north, driven by someone he'd got in touch with through the message board. At more or less the last possible moment, I made my mind up to go; the die cast, I went to the pub with my partner and got slurringly, irresponsibly drunk. We fell asleep at three: at half-past six my alarm woke me, shuddering the bedside table. I staggered through a still-dark Camberwell to Denmark Hill, finding myself on a northbound train an hour later by way of Victoria and Euston. A wintry sun came up over the Chilterns, and I tried to read a novel, realising swiftly that I hadn't yet sobered up. This was confirmed by the rambling incoherence I presented to my brother when he picked me up, took us back to his house for a swift cup of tea, and drove us to the junction where our rendezvous had been arranged.

Soon enough a hatchback, its front seats occupied by two men in strips from former seasons, pulled in and drove straight over to us. We got out as they did, exchanging slightly reticent greetings. It was P's car. P was the same age as me, and fitted the profile – wry, self-deprecatingly ironic – of many live-away Darlingtonians I'd met. He'd driven from the South Coast, stopping near Bristol to pick up K, who'd travelled from Wales. K was older and, surprisingly, had no firm connection with Darlington beyond having been born on a nearby military base. He'd started supporting the club in the Nineties for what seemed slightly hard-to-fathom reasons, maintaining contact through the fanzine network and, more recently, online. He was taciturn, in a good-humoured way, and concerned he wouldn't know anyone when he got to Barrow.

I can't drive, and my brother's insurance turned out on last-minute inspection not to be comprehensive, so we tucked into the back seat as K took over at the wheel. Coming into Staffordshire, rain and sleet hammered the windscreen and carriageway as wagons churned up water. If the geography was right for the occasion, the pathetic fallacy was also playing its part, setting up an appropriately muddy endgame. We passed fans of other clubs flying their scarves from rear windows, and swapped stories of away-day unruliness and adolescent memories of Feethams. Most of the players we talked about were mentioned at first because of their stunning inability or their dogged commitment to causes that weren't so much lost as buried, fossilised and on the coal-heap. A few, we agreed, had seemed fantastic, but would have been well out of their depth just a level or so higher.

Nowadays, when you don't travel to football, it's easy enough to forget that anybody else does. Newspapers tend to presume that they're speaking to an audience whose main engagement with the game comes through the television; walking past many pubs on a Saturday lunchtime or Sunday evening, you could be forgiven for thinking that the barstool had replaced the terrace as the main vantage point for spectating. At two on a Saturday afternoon not long before the trip to Barrow, I saw a man in a Manchester United scarf walking away from my East Dulwich local, bereft of companions but in all other respects bearing the exact pose – one that belies a realisation that the weekend's over, and that it's time to return home for tea and thoughts of Monday – with which L.S. Lowry's figures comport themselves leaving a stadium. The internet has accentuated this shift: one can now indulge in all the rage and disappointment that accompanies watching a match without having to visibly confront other teams' supporters in the flesh, an act which once revealed them as a more or less identical band of hopeful, desiring, overjoyed or embittered individuals to one's fellow-travellers. Stop going to games for more than a few months, in other words, and you may well begin to think that the game has become virtual, hyperreal, deterritorialised – the adjectival theoretical keywords, in fact, used to describe much contemporary experience.

That, however, would be to ignore the surprisingly large number of people who persist in attending matches. A weekend's aggregate gate in the Premier League is in the region of 350,000, and even down at the tenth and eleventh levels, an individual division can clock a thousand or so paying customers on a Saturday. Although internet-age distancing effects encroach on the match – note how many supporters now watch a penalty or even corner through their phone viewfinder – attendances are not only robust, but well up on twenty-five years ago. With the media regarding their constituency as television fans, however, to be an actually-attending supporter can feel like full-blown recusancy.

This was certainly the case at Barrow, where we finally arrived following an error that took us towards Lake Windermere and a long tailback on the single-carriageway road going into the town. Above Holker Street, the football ground, as the land rises away from the coastal plain, there are terraced Victorian houses arranged in wide wind-tunnels of streets; the flatter ground, however, has been taken up with new development. In an Asda car-park, P, who'd taken on the driving at Lancaster, backed into a local woman doing her Saturday lunchtime shop. Bucking the trend towards crisis that was starting to characterise things, nothing was scratched; we escaped with a telling-off, resolving to park and get on our feet.

That didn't take long, and we entered Barrow's clubhouse buildings to buy a drink. There's a contemporary British artist called Mike Nelson who makes maze-like installation pieces which investigate and play with the lived environments of groups operating on the margins of consumer society: biker gangs, terrorist organisations, traffickers. His most famous work, *The Coral Reef*, exhibited in Pimlico's Tate Britain for a few years, drew its audience into a series of dusty, badly lit rooms connected by undecorated corridors full of exposed plumbing and unfinished joinery. The rooms all gave the impression of having been immediately deserted; fled, perhaps, on a tip-off revealing the imminent encroachment of the authorities. It played with the clichés and iconography of modern-day insurgency: humming Celeron desktops with dial-up Internet, calendars marked in non-Latin alphabets, half-empty food tins. This was the most explicit of Nelson's unnerving spaces, but it fitted into the general pattern of his work in that it gave us a place which was simultaneously inside and outside the contemporary world, a hollowing out, one might say, of the boundary between the 20th and the 21st centuries. The clubhouses of the vast majority of non-league football clubs in the UK could be vacated and then transplanted in their entirety into art galleries and then passed off as works by the same artist. Adverts for wedding hire in early-version Windows fonts, trophies from county cup competitions and pre-season tournaments in the Channel Islands or Gibraltar, function rooms with PAs and school-disco lighting rigs. The suggestion, once again, is of a world which persists furtively, just under the stainless-steel skin of the contemporary.

The innards of Holker Street offered no exception to this rule. I managed to get lost on several occasions – as I have in Nelson's installations – following the noise of the concentration of fans who had crossed the Pennines only to find myself at the dead end of a flock-wallpapered corridor covered in old youth-team photographs and enticements to enter raffles or attend karaoke nights. Finally working my way upstairs to the bar, wide windows looked out across the muddy, balding pitch and let in the watery sky of Westmorland. Hangovers have always seemed to exaggerate my sense experiences, at their worst – or, to tell the truth, their best – giving them the lysergic charisma of a trip without the sanctimonious flower-power fluorescence. The sudden panorama through the window of the *echt* north, the smell of a carpet doused repeatedly in cheap keg bitter, the mild claustrophobia of a room not really designed for such numbers, the acoustically merging dialects of south Durham and Furness came together in an emotional jolt that I couldn't quite rationalise or reduce to a single cause.

Finishing our drinks, my brother and I left the fans we'd driven up with and went to find an old friend in the queue for the turnstiles. The line was stretching back down the street behind the main stand; a simple, thousand-seat structure with a roof painted cheerfully in the home side's blue and white. After going through the gate, we took our place along with one thousand other Darlington fans on the open terrace behind the goal to the right of the structure: the Barrow fans were filling its seats and the covered standing area opposite it. The wind had picked up further and the balls both teams' players were now hoofing around in the warm-up were catching in the watery gusts, hanging in the air and coming back down at unpredictable trajectories.

As the teams came onto the pitch to start the match, the Cumbrian fans in the paddock to our left hoisted a large banner emblazoned with the words "A FOOTBALL CLUB IS FOR LIFE, NOT JUST FOR CHRISTMAS". Recognition of the gesture passed through our section, not exactly gradually, but not instantaneously either: the structure of the moment felt cinematic, yet another feature of a day which had been preordained as one to remember and which was not going to be allowed to lose that status regardless of whatever happened on the field. A few of the Darlington players chatted to fans behind the goal, expressing thanks that so many had made the journey. The imminent oblivion of the club clearly mattered to them in a fashion which gave the lie to the notion that footballers are mechanically money-driven and unresponsive to those who pay to watch them. That on this occasion they dealt with the trauma of pending extinction with smiles and jokes was appreciated: their level-headed generosity was striking given that, in a very real sense, their livelihoods depended on the club. At the fifth level of the English game, an abrupt cessation of pay is not something dealt with easily, and it's easy to understand why some players working at the boundaries of professional and semi-professional football choose the second of these options, using the sport as a secondary income to top up a more reliable wage from elsewhere.

Of course, precariousness has a marked effect on the pitch. The half was not long gone when our weakened team conceded its first goal, failing to clear a ball spinning down in the wind and then giving Barrow's egregiously competent centre-forward space to whip a shot in from the edge of the penalty area. Fifteen minutes later, just after the half hour, their lead was doubled as a cross came in from the left, sat on an updraft for longer than it had any ballistic right to, and was met by the other striker's head. On the away terrace, hopes that Darlington's existence could end on a victory were quickly being moderated to accommodate the clear gap in ability and morale between the teams. A goal was all we wanted now. By halftime, it had failed to materialise, with our threat limited to some pretty but toothless passing movements in the half of the hosts. However, the mood at the break was largely unaffected by the score, with the main area of concern how we were supposed to respond come the final whistle, regardless of the result. Some thought the fans should go onto the pitch to congratulate the players for sticking with such an obviously lost cause for several months; others felt it was the responsibility of the players to come and thank us.

Quarter of an hour after the restart, with the night coming up over the sea from the south not quite having consumed the last of the wintery sky, the contest was ended after a Barrow winger got round the back of the Darlington defence and a leg – no one was quite clear whether it belonged to a home or away player – diverted the ball, which trickled over the line, just out of reach of Sam Russell, the Teesside-born goalkeeper who had made over two hundred appearances in two spells at the club. A reliable performer, Russell enjoyed a more than usually good rapport with the fans, and was very near the top of the list of players who didn't deserve to be in this situation. He slammed his palms into the mud of the goalmouth, half-heartedly chastised the young defenders who had made the series of mistakes leading to the goal, and picked the ball out of the net, acknowledging the increasingly droll irony from the fans immediately behind the goal with a half-smile. The afternoon was drawing to a close, but in the manner of scores of defeats I'd weathered with the club in the past: an atmosphere which had suddenly been drained of its sense of funereal purpose. This was little more than Typical Darlo, albeit with a little less moaning and a bit more singing. I started looking around for something I could lock onto which would return me to the condition of emotional febrility I'd been in earlier on, noting a pair of young children with their faces painted in black and white hoops and deciding I'd try and find them at the final whistle. The tears were apparently going to need dragging out. Stewards in hi-vis jackets had formed a cordon in front of the Darlington fans as a hundred or so teenagers massed at the front, determined to get onto the pitch in line with the tradition that had been respected at the final game of every season since I'd started going, whether or not it had been a good campaign. Some, you knew, would be long-time fans; others had certainly come along for the ride, looking for an excuse to get out of their Saturday routines, not wanting to miss out on any action. My brother railed at them, knowing that, if they went on, the players wouldn't be allowed to come and say goodbye, but on they went as soon as the referee blew his whistle.

Night had come in properly now and the majority of fans who had not gone onto the pitch milled around in responsive confusion. Some were cursing the selfishness of the invaders, others were trying to get songs started, many were simply talking to matchday friends, wondering whether or not there'd be occasion to meet in the future. I sought out the face-painted children and felt my eyes prickle, but the catharsis I'd been expecting and hoping for didn't come. We walked out of the ground, where a few Darlington fans were still arguing with stewards, saw our friend to his car and found our travelling companions for the journey back to the Midlands. On the motorway, we talked and joked a bit, keeping an eye on Twitter as speculation filtered through that the club would find a way of surviving until the end of the season, regardless of what happened after that.

I've not seen or spoken to K or P since that trip, even on the Internet. It's a long and convoluted story, perhaps even more so than that of how the club came to be in such a perilous situation in the first place, but Darlington were, at the very last, spared until the end of the season – although they still finished bottom of the league, hopelessly. In the summer of 2012, the Quakers were told that, in order to carry on playing senior football, they'd have to reform under a different name in the Northern League, a minor competition for sides from the North East. Games were moved to nearby Bishop Auckland's compact stadium, and Darlington 1883, as they are now listed in newspapers, have still to return to their namesake town, despite achieving two promotions in three seasons and having set out plans to share a small stadium near the now overgrown site of Feethams with a local rugby club. The trip to Cumbria, then, felt anticlimactic in a fashion which actually turned out to be somewhat appropriate, a haphazardly sentimental attempt to mark an ending which was in two senses – because the club saw out the season, and because the club reformed – not really an ending.

If the day was, for me, marked and perhaps marred by its ultimate lack of resolution, it did bring certain other things into clear relief. The most significant of these was something which had been nagging at me for a long time, beginning in my teens. It is often flippantly proclaimed that the beauty, even the *truth* of football, lies in its universality: it is a sport which can be played with the most minimal equipment, and it can be adapted to nearly any environment. Played globally, it provides an instant conversational opening in such a wide variety of social scenarios it seems pointless to begin listing examples. Against this, however, football is a scene of an intense particularity which would, at first glance, appear to be something which contrasts such universality. Every experience of matchgoing I have had has been rooted intensely in place; even if some of those experiences have involved an encounter with a sudden evacuation of the feeling of locatedness, the sudden sense of placelessness is heightened by the awareness of locality which preceded it. I cannot tell a story about going to watch Barrow play Darlington in late winter in West Cumbria with sole, or even predominant, recourse to a vocabulary of the universal: without the social colour, there would be virtually nothing to say.

This, then, is what some might see as the paradox, but I'd prefer to regard as a productive dialectic, of football: between genuine universality and a situated, historical specificity that can't be transposed or transplanted. Somehow, the understanding that the activity with which we choose to fill our Saturday afternoon is an activity pursued from Kamchatka to Buenos Aires, or along any other axis we might draw, is one which elicits the local and makes the sport an ideal receptacle for communal meanings and memories. On one hand, it signifies absolute, pan-global sameness. On the other, it throws up an infinite number of unique, unrepeatable events. Our love for the game is not by any means anchored in that mutually intelligible thing which happens on the pitch, because it is just as much, and almost certainly more so, a derivation of its intersection with our social and political lives.

# CHAPTER ONE

# "The One Moment, the One Match": Football Modernism

> But even at that moment he had a dim foreboding that this
> happier frame of mind was also not normal.
> – FYODOR DOSTOEVSKY, *Crime and Punishment*

> The message came from the manager and the fans: "Don't relax
> just because you've won a few now." You win something and you
> say, "It's gone", and then you move on.
> – ROY KEANE, *The Second Half*

There's a YouTube clip that I've been really fond of over the past
few years. It's footage from a mid-season friendly between the
Istanbul club Galatasaray SC, globally notorious for the fervent,
sometimes excessive zeal of their supporters, and VFR Aalen, then
of the German second division. The match itself is nothing more
than an excuse for the teams' managers to keep their players fit
during a winter break, or to cast an eye over reserves, and, unu-
sually, given the level of passion Galatasaray's fans will bring to
the most meaningless of occasions, the stands are barren. In the
video, it's just after halftime and those who have bothered to turn
up have yet to witness a goal. The visiting goalkeeper punts a long
kick upfield – the viewer suspects this has been a recurring strategy in the game – and a centre-back rises to head clear, overcoming
the most half-hearted of aerial challenges from the target of the
ball. As the attack is repelled, two cream-white shapes appear on
the bottom of the screen, moving towards the action. The camera

26

quickly zooms in to focus on a pair of young Labradors, tussling over a discarded newspaper as they incur onto the pitch. The referee halts play as he notices the dogs, and the players begin to crowd around the animals, bending down to pet them. Stewards enter the field; a player passes a retriever to one of them. The crowd, such as it is, applauds the interruption, and the camera follows the intruders as they are removed from the field of play. In the most touching moment of the clip, the dog who holds the newspaper drops it in the course of being carried away, and looks ruefully back towards the object as the referee convenes a drop ball so play can restart.

My enjoyment of the clip is really only a synecdoche of what it is that draws me to football in the first place, and I will return to this subject in another chapter. For now, I want to talk a little about how I used it as a classroom metaphor to explain an idea from critical theory and, more particularly, what interested me about how my students (and colleagues, and friends) responded to this usage. A month or so after I first saw the film, I had to give a lecture for first-year students which introduced them to the ideas of Jacques Lacan. Few eighteen year-olds have encountered Lacan's work, and those who have tend to be familiar only with his early ideas on the mirror stage. The aim of the lecture was to get them thinking in terms of the three "orders" – the Symbolic, the Imaginary and the notoriously ineffable Real – which, according to his thought, compose both human inner experience and the entire fabric of the social. Searching for a visual illustration of how these orders engage one another, I thought of the dogs on that frosty evening in Istanbul. The match itself, I thought, approximated Lacan's Symbolic, a finite set of rules which, like language, may give rise to a wide, but not limitless, variety of outcomes. The colours of the teams' shirts and the (admittedly muted) songs of the supporters, meanwhile, seemed to resemble the Imaginary, the false sense of unity and wholeness towards which the Symbolic, ultimately vainly, orients itself: think of the footballing cliché about "playing for the shirt". Finally, the intruding dogs index the Real, the trauma which the Imaginary denies and which eludes the capture of the Symbolic – the civic, regional or patriotic "glory" which is the nominal stake of a match is precisely opposed by this farce, and the event reminds us of the expressive finitude of the rules.

Lacanian *tifosi* will probably want to point out the flaws in this analogy (there are some, albeit sketchy, rules about foreign bodies, for example) but, in the pedagogic context, it served its purpose, or appeared to have done so come the end of the semester. But it isn't the precision of the comparison that bothers me so much as the nuances of the response it received. While there was no doubt in the minds of the students that the subject matter was serious, something to be *understood* and *learned*, the vehicle of the metaphor was almost immediately taken as a piece of conspiratorial frivolity designed to engage precisely due to the fact it could be read as throwaway. In other words, it was perceived as an attempt on my part to say something like, "look, you can understand Lacan's orders in lots of ways, many of which are silly, and here's an example which is particularly silly, because it's drawn from football". I find that whenever football is drawn upon for material out of which a simile can be manufactured, there's an aspect of comedy driven by the supposedly shared recognition that it is the foolish Other to art, philosophy, love, finance or anything else which engages the intellect or subtler passions. The opposition between seriousness and frivolity has itself, very famously, been a source of comedy in the form of *Monty Python*'s Philosophers' Football Match, where the (Ancient) Greeks narrowly edge out Germany with a late goal from Socrates.

Steven Connor's *Philosophy of Sport* opens with an investigation of the apparent dichotomy between intellectual work and sport. As he puts it, an analysis of the "parallels between sport and philosophy" is desirable "perhaps precisely because each is [...] so obviously the absolute other to the other". Connor's phenomenology of sport in this book is fascinating, but I want to quibble his insistence on treating sport as a category possessing "essential unity". My belief is that football, in its totality, is phenomenologically specific, an experience which – if we step out of the limiting boundaries of considering it as something which one *plays* – is emphatically separate from other sports. The reasons for this, I want to argue, are subjects for the treatment of sociological, historical and political analysis, but not confined by such approaches, and a grasp of the game's uniqueness is as likely to come by asking the kinds of questions of it literary critics or even psychoanalysts trade in. A poetics of football which tries to give a proper account of the way that its force and allure lie in nothing other than the caesura between "the game itself" and its adjunctive culture is already implicitly political, but it's my belief that these politics can be drawn out to demonstrate how such radicality can be considered in a way which goes beyond a sociology of its audience. Supporters are a hugely significant part of football's difference from the *lumpen* mass of "sport", and one of my main concerns here is to define what it is they *do* in a historical moment where that *doing* is being reduced to televisual spectating. Nevertheless, academic sociological studies are prone to missing vital formal and aesthetic features, even within fan culture itself.

I attended my first football match in the autumn of 1990, just after the World Cup in Italy which saw an initially unpromising England side reach the semi-finals. Unlike many fans, my younger brother and I were initially taken by my mother – who still attends occasionally – although, after a couple of months of trips to watch Darlington, my father started to come with us instead. My mum had a habit of ironising the fact she was at the match, a routine which involved dramatising the boredom and cold and discomfort, which I suppose meant that no component of football could ever, in those formative weeks, have the mythological stability of what Roland Barthes, in *Mythologies*, calls "the what goes without saying". There's a scene in B.S. Johnson's manically experimental revenge comedy *Christie Malry's Own Double-Entry* which addresses the manner in which football is something whose givens new fans are supposed to accept immediately:

> "My father", said Headlam, "took me into a pub on my fifteenth birthday, stuck a pint of bitter in my hand and said: 'Like all men in this family, son, you do three things as a matter of course – you drink bitter, vote Labour, and support Chelsea.' The bitter took some getting used to, as I'd been drinking brown up till then, but I was a Chelsea man already."

*Christie Malry* is a study of how values are assigned and norms created, not least by fiction itself, and this scene is instrumental in tipping the reader the wink about what is going on. A Chelsea fan who harboured his own aspirations of playing professionally before embarking on a strange, and ultimately tragic, career of post-Beckettian writing and leftfield filmmaking, Johnson's books wrangle with common sense and seek to strip bare its absurdities. Here, the choice of a football team (and, by extension, the choice to attend football in the first place) is shown to be a pure "matter of course" which does not permit questions, and it's a deft illustration of how it takes its part in the formation of (particularly male) identities. Of course, one of the things which might be identified as "good" about football is the way in which it can prompt identification with the collective, but it is also clearly the case that the treating of it as an inevitability, or a set of inevitabilities, means that for many it's something that has come to be associated with the maintenance of a political, social and even aesthetic status quo.

What happens, though, if the kind of teasing or joking which draws to the surface some of its absurdities is something which is, by some strange paradox, built into football itself? Is it possible that the sport so often dismissed as a social opiate, the rise of which was suspiciously coterminous with that of industrial capitalism and its concomitant need to regulate large concentrations of people, actually has a more interesting – and less straightforwardly instrumental – relationship with power? Could it even lay claim to its own internal critique of power? Is it possible that, like modernist art, literature and music, football is (at least in part) an outcome of industrial capital's assertion of hegemonic control in the middle of the 19th century which exists in a *necessarily* contradictory relationship with it?

There's a beguiling historical accident here, although it shouldn't be reduced to the status of mere coincidence. In 1863, the poet and essayist Charles Baudelaire published, in serial form in *Figaro*, a long essay titled 'Le peintre de la vie moderne', rendered later in English as 'The Painter of Modern Life'. The essay purported to be a study of, and tribute to, the watercolourist Constantin Guys, regarded by Baudelaire as a gallant documenter of the specifically modern and a crucial (if minor) naysayer to the assumptions of the academies, but it extended far beyond its reach and served as a *cri de coeur* for an art which grubbied its hands with capitalist modernity. Baudelaire's genius here was to recognise in Guys a capacity for capturing the true spirit of the modern: he was "the painter of the passing moment and of all the suggestions of eternity it contains". Modernity, on these terms, is something which is simultaneously composed of the fleeting, contingent or disposable, and the eternal, but the latter is unlocked only by the mysterious graces of the former. Indeed, Baudelaire's own poetry suggests it is the very transience of modern experience which makes a vision of the eternal possible; the eternal, in other words, emerges in its negation or impossibility. One of his most powerful articulations of this comes in 'À une passante'/'In Passing', a lyric which commemorates an extremely brief encounter on a busy boulevard:

> The traffic roared around me, deafening!
> Tall, slender, in mourning – noble grief –
> a woman passed, and with a jewelled hand
> gathered up her black embroidered hem;
>
> stately yet lithe, as if a statue walked...
> And trembling like a fool, I drank from eyes
> as ashen as the clouds before a gale
> the grace that beckons and the joy that kills.
>
> Lightening...then darkness! Lovely fugitive
> whose glance has brought me back to life! But where
> is life – not this side of eternity?
>
> Elsewhere! Too far, too late, or never at all!
> Of me you know nothing, I nothing of you – you
> whom I might have loved and who knew that too!

Eternity is what *does not* happen, but (urbanised) life is composed of a series of events which, in their repetitive evocation of this not-happening, point insistently towards it. Existence in industrial, urbanised modernity is a prolonged exercise in trying to make these glimpses of eternity intelligible after the fact: poetry is transformed from the aestheticisation of feelings which once had approximated eternity into the aestheticisation of the way in which feelings denote the absence of the eternal. Walter Benjamin's take on Baudelaire's sort-of-missed encounter has it as a fast-fading illustration of "love – not at first sight, but at last sight", suggesting how eternity is always that which is disappearing in the figurative rear-view mirror. Gone are the regulated certainties of pre-industrial life, replaced by the immutable fact that experience is a constant slithering away of the meaningful. Baudelaire's modernity is "the ephemeral, the fugitive, the contingent", and those who neglect this fact "cannot fail to tumble into the abyss of an abstract and indeterminate beauty". 'The Painter of Modern Life' serves as a manifesto for art which rejects "abstract and indeterminate" notions in favour of concentrating on the concrete finitudes of modern being, which, by necessity, implies a resolve to embrace transience as the cornerstone of the aesthetic.

Both 'The Painter of Modern Life' and Baudelaire's poetry hinge on a decisive shift in social patterns that took place as urbanisation heralded a climate in which the parochial, with its relative predictability, ceased to form the basis of most people's experience. Where once the lived environment was defined by familiarity between individuals and its attendant sense of time by the seasonal exigencies of agriculture, urban dwelling meant a constant chain of unrepeatable encounters with people who would never again be met and a more diurnal appreciation of temporality arranged by industrial and clerical work. A structuring tension of modernity, then, is the play between its accentuated haphazardness and its equally pointed rationalisation: the elevation of clock time above time determined "naturally" represented a standardisation of life, but also created apertures for random events which resisted repetition. Work became absolutely, frequently painfully, repetitive, but the interdependency of different spheres of capitalist work drew workplaces into a conurbative proximity that produced populations of a size which by statistical necessity made most people strangers to one another.

Baudelaire's essay was his contribution to making this new situation into the grounds for a novel aesthetic. Another text which came together in 1863, however, shows us that it was not only art which was in the process of radical reinvention. In October of that year, a committee of public schoolmasters met in Cambridge

33

to review an earlier set of rules, drawn up in 1848, for the game of football. The 1863 Cambridge Rules were agreed weeks before the first meeting of the Football Association above a pub near Covent Garden, where a number of representatives of London schools and clubs agreed to adopt them as standard. This standardisation must be seen as the beginning of what we recognise as the modern game but, beyond that, we might identify in it an inadvertent statement of intent which did for the sport what Baudelaire did for modernist aesthetics.

What were the immediate consequences of this codification? Primarily, I think, it opened the door to football becoming a spectator sport in the contemporary sense of that term. A standard set of rules meant that people in disparate places recognised they were watching a game that others were also watching elsewhere, which transformed it into a communicative currency effective across geographical distances which increased as the laws were accepted in ever-more far-flung places. This gave form to competitions with objectives which were increasingly long-term, at least when compared to the immediate priority of winning an individual match for the sake of a school's, or village's, honour. Correspondingly, the duration of football altered from that of the match, whose temporality was purely tactical, to that of the campaign or – a little further down the line – season, which needed to be thought of in a mix of tactical (*how to win the game*) and strategic (*how to win games repeatedly*) registers.

The sport thereby acquired an interest-value which slipped the tether of the instant but, paradoxically, shunted its emphasis from the eternalised "indeterminate beauty" of playing to win in the name of abstractions such as honour and sportsmanship to the "ephemeral, the fugitive, the contingent". Victory, as football fans know, epitomises fleetingness: as the cliché goes, a team or player is "only as good as [their] last game" in a competitive structure where a seemingly epic win can be dampened almost immediately by a chastening defeat. The same holds for competitions themselves, which, at least in the case of domestic leagues and cups, conclude and restart at intervals which rarely take up more than a couple of months. The cup win that is followed by a first-round exit the following season, and the promotion that is followed by a humiliating relegation are hard facts of the sport with which most are familiar.

It is in this sense that football fans, and arguably players and managers, experience ecstasy "not at first sight, but at last sight". The moment at which victory is sealed is simultaneously the one at which it begins to recede into the past, to become memory; indeed, it is something which is memorialised in the very instance of its happening, or even *before* it occurs. The desire to win a competition, it seems, is frequently less to do with the fact of winning than with the anticipation of the memory of winning; the fear of not winning is predominantly a fear of not having a memory of winning, which is, therefore, also a fear of not having a memory of anticipating the dwindling of victory's emotional loot! Amongst other things, Baudelaire's poetics looked to formalise a way in which art can testify to the temporal complexity of feeling in modernity; the standardisation of football's rules gave the game a poetic architecture which produces that same complexity. The quote from *Crime and Punishment* which serves as an epigraph to this chapter might be borrowed to denote the manner in which football fandom is an experience which does not *involve* anxiety, but which is constituted in its entirety by it. Any sense of completion which the game affords is shadowed by the awareness that this sense is illusory and contingent and, indeed, the primary satisfaction offered by football is inescapably coloured with morbidity and perversity, a pleasure taken in the anticipation of approaching unpleasure.

Alongside the development of competitive structures which made possible the looping temporality of supporters' desire, standardisation also gave rise to the conditions which under-pinned the beginning of football's commodification. While we can look at the history of most football clubs founded in the 19th century in order to note that they often began as associations of workers or developed out of similarly communitarian structures such as church groups, it took very little time for teams to fall into the hands of businessmen. The fact of a support base who main-tained a long-standing interest in the fortunes of a club meant that, in any given case, there was a readymade group of customers who wished to witness these fortunes by attending games and which could, consequently, have a price put on it. It's in this that the ongoing dialectical tension of football emerges.

Generally, the ownership of football clubs resembles a scale model of capitalism as Marx saw it. By repeatedly and predicta-bly, as opposed to sporadically and whimsically, going to watch a club, supporters lend to it an identity which exceeds that consti-tuted by those, namely the players, immediately implicated by the match. This identity, this thing, which is now more than a group of people playing a game, becomes a product, a commodity made so *by none other than the people who buy it*. However, it is largely the case, not least in the United Kingdom, that the product is owned by a limited number of people with the financial wherewithal to purchase a stake in it. The football "experience", which, since the early days, has centered on paying to fuse briefly with an incom-plete competitive process of which the match itself forms only a part, is sold back to those who generate it in the first place; fur-thermore, the loyalty of fans allows for a monopolistic control over things such as ticket prices. Barring the occasional conflu-ences of interest that occur when proverbial local-boys-made-good take over their childhood teams, the relationship between supporters and club owners is by its nature an antagonistic one between producers and those who have their hands on the means of production.

This has, of course, been satirised by fans for decades. "Why do I pay to watch that rubbish every week?" is not just something supporters say, but something that those with no interest in football caricature supporters as saying. To the outsider – and, indeed, to some modern fans, but we'll come to that later – this is a virtually inscrutable aspect of supporting which is one of the incarnate forms of football's preposterousness. But the fan who actually does ask the question has historically always really known the answer to it – they go for the very reason that they *can* ask the question, allowing them to be on the inner fold of the absurdity of taking part in an activity whose opportunities for sustained pleasure, in the uncomplicated sense, are scarce. Football fans have, or at least had, a handle on what modernist time was all about, specifically the melancholy way in which happiness is something which occurs at "last sight". This understanding, which ranges from the tacit to the explicit, gives rise to solidarities of irony which are grounded in the fleeting character of success and deny abstract ideals. Furthermore, it is in these solidarities that the radical possibility of football begins.

Before exploring this, however, there needs to be a firm restatement of the idea that football's aesthetics and politics are immanent to the sport, so long as it can be agreed that it is a *spectator* sport. The last few decades have seen several literary attempts, so to speak, to rescue football from itself that have concentrated on presenting matchgoing as something which it is permissible for the culturally-aware to do. In Britain at least, none of these have had more far-reaching effects than Nick Hornby's memoir *Fever Pitch*, published serendipitously in 1992, just as English football was starting to lay claim to a new prosperity in the wake of the 1990 World Cup and the waning of hooliganism. Hornby's work was a *tour-de-force* in cheese-course conviction which insisted that a life well-lived could accommodate both a comprehensive understanding of John Updike's erotic worldview and trips to Highbury to watch Arsenal: its harshest critics suggested it was a manual designed to assist *Guardian* readers in justifying the fact that they occasionally tuned into *Match of the Day*. An answer to those who alleged that football was either a pointless waste of time or a pernicious vehicle of false consciousness, it positively revelled in football's primitivism, situating it in opposition to, say, theatre or art cinema.

This supposed dichotomy, rather than Hornby's mooted inauthenticity as a football fan, was what really undermined *Fever Pitch*. The hardest-to-swallow aspect of the book was its belief that football was an arena in which men, regardless of their class or education, could safely play out their deep masculinity. A persistent motif is that, once inside a football ground, the author would speak and behave in a way in which he would never dream of in his "real" life. Football, therefore, was positioned as a potential safety valve for guaranteeing, amongst other things, a particular form of bourgeois domesticity, and was depicted as a space in which aggressive energies could be theatricalised. That there is a cathartic element to attending, or simply watching, matches is something that seems to be beyond doubt, but stressing this excessively serves to uncritically preserve the somewhat weathered opposition between football and what is taken to be genuinely worthy of "intelligent" attention. Indeed, whereas a substantial amount of the literature which has occurred around the game since the 1980s has concentrated on soothing the anxieties a middle-class constituency may have about it, earlier cultural depictions of the subject have recognised in it something which goes beyond a simple, permissible, guilty catharsis, and resisted the temptation to portray it as "working-class theatre" or some comparably belittling soubriquet.

In these representations, football is not made into the Other of high culture, but identified as the only possible way in which a certain set of ideas can be expressed. The closing passages of

Henry Green's 1929 novel *Living* – one of Britain's great interwar "proletarian" fictions, written, surprisingly, by an upper-class aesthete – give some sense of this, as two factory workers go to watch Aston Villa:

> Gates and Connolly pass in and stand on the mound, they go to behind the goalposts and lean against rail there. Silver band in dark blue overcoats is playing in middle of the green, green pitch. Everything but the grass is black with smoke, only thin blue waves of smoke coming up from the dark crowds already gives any colour, and the pink brick.
>
> Band plays and always, at the gates, men are coming in, lines of them coming in thicker and thicker. Man with a rattle lets this off suddenly, then suddenly stops. Drunk man begins shouting at this. Now as this mound is filling up you see nothing but faces, lozenges, against black shoulders. As time gets nearer so more rattles are let off, part of the crowd begins singing. The drunk man, who has a great voice, roars and shouts and near him hundreds of faces are turned to look at him. The band packs up, it moves off, then over at further corner the whole vast crowd that begins roaring, the Villa team comes out, then everyone is shouting. On face of the two mounds great swaying, like corn before wind, is made down towards the ground, frantic excitement. Gates wailed and sobbed for now his voice had left him. The Villa, the Villa, come on the Villa. Mr Connolly stood transfixed with passion and 30,000 people waved and shrieked and swayed and clamoured at eleven men who play the best football in the world. These took no notice of the crowd, no notice.

*Living* is, quite apart from its significance as an experimental novel, still a notable literary curio in that it represents the work of an author of considerable economic and social privilege depicting working-class experience sympathetically (in the truest sense of that word) and without imposing an unwieldy anthropological frame. This is not, in other words, George Orwell heading for Wigan with his interpretative coordinates already programmed: instead, the writing gives its milieu considerable space to breathe unencumbered by extraneous proselytising. It deals almost purely in sense experience, albeit the sense experience of a disembodied narrator, and descriptions of movement, of the desire lines within a football ground. This is the surge of the crowd in all its stirring ambiguity: "great swaying, like corn before wind, is made down towards the ground, frantic excitement". Green neither charges the crowd, as so many bourgeois idealists did at the time, with revolutionary responsibility, nor finds in it any conspicuous threat. The energy is focused on the match itself. To repurpose a term conceived by blogger Splintering Bone Ashes, this could be regarded as the energy of "negative solidarity". In its original coinage, which I will return to later in this book, "negative solidarity" describes a politically unhelpful working-class solidarity which develops not around a mutual sense of class interest, but around antagonism towards a scapegoat such as "immigrants", or "benefit scroungers". In this instance, however, "negative" does not describe a solidarity which inverts its own key principle, but the *object* of solidarity: circuitously, the match has no intrinsic positive terms, possessing meaning only by the grace of what it generates extrinsically.

Something else interesting is at work here. While the spectators wave and shriek and sway and are "transfixed with passion", the players take "no notice of the crowd, no notice". Although Green's writing is known for seducing itself into gorgeous redundancy with the non-signifying pleasure of prosodic and acoustic effects, the repetition here feels insistent, an attempt to tell the reader something, namely that there is a disjuncture between the crowd, who focus their desire on the game, and the players of the game, whose desire is internalised by the match. This *should* remind us that the game itself is self-contained, that it is onto-logically separate from its social milieu, but it somehow does the opposite, highlighting how this separateness is a mere contingency, an act of wilful "not noticing". Likewise, the transfixion of the crowd's desire by the game is not a given: that energy could be unhitched, refocused, directed elsewhere. This passage stands, I think, as an early ironic dismissal of the idea that football can simply be separated off from its environment and packaged cleanly and neatly as a leisure commodity. The surreptitious call-back to Ezra Pound's micropoem 'In a Station of the Metro' ("The apparition of these faces in the crowd; / Petals on a wet, black bough") in Green's "faces, lozenges, against black shoulders", serves to remind us that football is a mere analogue of the apparitional aspect of modernity, but one which can, at its best, when not treated as a mere sporting distraction, offer a critical perspective on that modernity. It is a site in which transience awaits mobilisation, even radicalisation.

Football and the modernist understanding of temporality are brought together in a more determined and rigorous way in B.S. Johnson's mesmerising and melancholic 1969 novel *The Unfortunates*, an undertaking renowned for its formal oddness. *The Unfortunates* is not bound in the way one typically expects: instead, it consists of a series of twenty-seven chapbooks which, with the exception of two marked "first" and "last", can be read in any order. This arrangement, one assumes, is designed to replicate the randomness of memory, its ability to shatter the present as an external stimulus suddenly makes an unprocessed experience of the past – a register of experience Benjamin calls *erlebnis* in his reading of Baudelaire – into *ehrfahrung*, something resolved and meaningful. Johnson's protagonist and narrator is a sportswriter who has been sent to a city, clearly Nottingham in the English East Midlands but not stated as such, to cover a match at the ground of a fictitious "City", seemingly modelled on Notts County FC.

Johnson was born in 1933 in London and left school at sixteen to work in a variety of clerical jobs, an experience which informs his satirical socialist metafiction *Christie Malry's Own Double-Entry*, which I have quoted above. However, he was able to attend King's College London after taking an adult education course, and published his first novel, *Travelling People*, in 1963. Despite sharing a working-class background with the Angry Young social realists of the time – his biography would lead one to expect a Southern Alan Sillitoe or David Storey – his literary touchstones were unashamedly experimental and modernist. While his writing is just as fixated as that of the postwar realists with the material experience of 1950s and 1960s Britain, he found ways of taking the tropes of that realism and turning them into the vehicles of a formal adventurousness that tended to question the very possibility of representation. In *The Unfortunates*, the realist trope flipped against itself is football.

Sport turns up insistently in postwar realism. Think of Storey's eminently filmable Camus-plays-Rugby-League *This Sporting Life*, or Sillitoe's miserabilist short story 'The Match', or the infamous football scenes in Barry Hines' *A Kestrel for a Knave*. As an occasional football reporter, sometime player, and dedicated Chelsea fan, Johnson was unlikely to be left out on this front, and his writing is packed with references to the game. There's the vignette from *Christie Malry* previously mentioned, a visit to Stamford Bridge in 1964's *Albert Angelo*, a downbeat drama of professional failure, and, of course, *The Unfortunates*.

In a *Guardian* article from June 2015 on the difficulties of making art of football, Barney Ronay mentioned *The Unfortunates* as one of the few works that had successfully extracted some aesthetic interest from the game. However, Ronay's description of the novel as a "wonderfully haunting" treatment of "loss and disintegration" suggests that football's role is basically incidental: the "central character [...] just happens to be a football reporter".

I would go further than this. Look, for example, at the opening passage:

> But I know this city! This green ticket-hall, the long office half-rounded at its ends, that ironic clerestory, brown glazed tiles, green below, the same, the decorative hammer-beams supporting nothing, above, of course! I know this city! How did I not realise when he said, Go and do City this weekend, that it was this city?

Here, the contingencies of football reporting – bearing in mind football's dialectic of the universal and the particular – can take you, unpredictably, *anywhere*, because the sport happens *everywhere*. Because of this, it can put us into an intimate encounter with loss, bringing us up against our past, against our investments "at last sight". More significantly, though, as I have argued above, football replays the whole drama of temporality in modernity, making it the very analogue of lost time. The description of the beginning of the match in particular makes explicit football's temporal modernism:

> Always, at the start of each match, the excitement, often the only moment of excitement, that this might be the ONE match, the match in which someone betters Payne's ten goals, where Hughie Gallacher after being floored nods one in while sitting down, where the extraordinary happens, something that makes it stand out, the match one remembers and talks about for years afterwards, the rest of one's life. The one moment, the one match. A new beginning, is it?

The contemporary football fan has become almost unaware of a discourse of "the memorable" surrounding the game, such is its media-based ubiquity. Commentators tell us repeatedly that a particular event – whether a moment of technical brilliance, an unthinkable underdog victory or a piece of Luis Suarez-style nefariousness – "will live long in the memory". Johnson seems to anticipate this hysteria here, but his version of "memory" does not really denote a place in which something "lives": rather, it is a recognition of the pastness, of the figurative "death" of the event itself. The writing appeals to the strange relationship between universality (or standardisation) and particularity (or unique-ness) which motivates both post-1863 football and modernism's conception of time: "each match" is characterised by something which "always" happens, namely the excitement about the pos-sibility of something *unique* taking place, which can be memo-rialised. For Johnson, though, the existence of memory is an acknowledgement of the hollowness of the present, of the lived-through, of *erlebnis* – we remember, and memorialise, because of a lack inherent in the moment of the event. In fact, the event only attains its form after the fact, once it is a done deal. Towards the end of the chapbook in which the match itself is covered, this is acknowledged when the difficulties of sportswriting are con-sidered. The protagonist says, "Now I must hack this into some shape, now I must make it into 500 well-chosen words. Yes, 500 they asked for."

Instead, then, of making football into a given, a device used to trope the possibility of stable acts of representation – the postwar realists made sport an icon of grittiness, a guarantor of truth-tell-ing – Johnson makes a candid association between the sport and modernism's identification of experience fragmented beyond the capabilities of representation. The role of football in the novel, then, is not an incidental one, not something added simply to give the literary experiment a splash of social colour: it is a fundamen-tal component of the experiment. The end of *The Unfortunates* makes this clear:

Paper, yes, Chelsea result.                Photo, pink football paper,
I thought that City bastard did that deliberately, this proves it, the
goalkeeper has the ball safely and Robbins still has his foot drawn
back to boot him              Chelsea result, down the bottom,
nearly, West Brom 1 Chelsea 1, oh, they could have done better, a
disappointment, still, it could have been worse, a draw, they must
just do better for the rest of the season. As indeed
About thirteen minutes to wait

This feels rather like a satire of the invariably downbeat endings
of the novels of Sillitoe, Storey, et al, but there is a little more to it.
Once again, we are instructed about the out-of-timeness of football, its belated aesthetic formalisation as something meaningful,
something which can be "proved" once it is no longer happening.
There is also a Baudelairean sense of the *what might have happened*, a retrospective acknowledgement of the potential of the
moment for producing different kinds of meaning, an investigation of lost possibility which is also a component of *ehrfahrung* in
Benjamin's account of 'In Passing'. Johnson, then, offers us a way
in which we can read football as a form of popular modernism,
reminding us of how Baudelaire's poetics (and Benjamin's gloss
on them) looked to formalise a way in which art can testify to the
temporal complexity of affective experience in modernity, and of
how the standardisation of football gave the game a poetic architecture which tracks and overlaps with that complexity.

The last author who might tell us something instructive about
the relationship between football and an aesthetics based on the
shifting time-sense of capitalism is the contemporary novelist
David Peace. Peace has published two football fictions, both about
era-defining managers of the British 1970s. The first, *The Damned
United*, narrates truculent Teessider Brian Clough's chaotic spell in
charge of a Leeds United shaped in the image of his arch-rival Don
Revie. *The Damned United* cites *The Unfortunates* as an influence in

its acknowledgements, and its depiction of time owes something to Johnson's fragmented technique. Alternate chapters focus on the first-person present, with Clough struggling to adapt to the clique culture at Leeds, and a second-person past, which narrates the miserable end of Clough's playing career and his early managerial successes at Hartlepool and Derby. Its trick is that the past can never quite catch up with the present, meaning that, however hard memory tries to recapitulate them – the second-person strikes the reader as Clough self-mythologising, as he was given to do – successes keep on slipping away. The 2009 film version of the novel, with Michael Sheen and Timothy Spall, turns the story into knockabout banter, a buddy comedy with rainy, brown-hued period detail, but it suffers from ditching the post-punk austerity of its source text, which imbues 1970s Yorkshire with a grimly expressionistic intensity. In his second football novel, 2013's *Red or Dead*, Peace deepens the gravity still further.

*Red or Dead* is, on one level, "about" Bill Shankly, the still-venerated manager who turned Liverpool from second-division also-rans into one of the dominant forces in European football. Some may choose to read it entirely on these terms, as a sporting novel set in the Merseyside of the Beatles and Gerry Marsden. Those who do so, however, are likely to be frustrated by the work's enormous length, its provocative use of repetition and its tendency to home in on the most minor of events with what is clearly a perverse level of detail. There is an almost idiotically minute grade of attentiveness:

> In the drive, in the car. In the night. Bill turned off the engine. In the night. Bill got out of the car. In the night. Bill walked up the drive. In the night. Bill unlocked the front door of the house. In the night. Bill opened the door. In the night. Bill stepped into the house. In the dark. Bill closed the door. In the dark. Bill put down his case in the hallway. In the dark. Bill walked down the hallway

to the kitchen. In the dark. Bill sat down at the table. In the dark.
Bill put his hand in his pocket. In the dark. Bill took out the chip.
The red and white chip. In the dark. Bill stared down at the chip.
The red and white chip. In the dark. Bill turned the chip in his fin-
gers. The red and white chip. In the dark.

This passage is by no means anomalous as an example of Peace's
rhythmic strategies and investment in banality in the novel. How
does one account for it? Some reviewers were led to read *Red or
Dead* as a tale of secular sainthood in which the reader is invited fully into the calm rigour of Shankly's interior world, thereby coming gradually to understand the patience that is intrinsic
to great acts. There is some truth in this reading, I think, but
it is worth bearing in mind that Peace had already tapped into
football's modernist time-perception in *The Damned United*, and
therefore reading *Red or Dead* as the continuation of a project of
formal experimentation begun in the earlier novel. Seen as such,
it comes to look more like a piece of durational art, an attempt
to show how time under capitalism encompasses not only the
Baudelairean explosion of experience, the unique moment's
destruction prior to its experiential completion, but the *weighti-
ness* of labour-time.

Football is not the same thing as art, and attempts to suggest it
is invariably become patronising. Nevertheless, as a form in which
experience is registered and made sense of, it shares certain parallels with modernist art which suggest how it is both a form of
practical modernism in itself and a useful structural metaphor *for*
modernity. My first experiences of experimental art either came
through or were mediated by football culture. Darlington's fanzine, a Xeroxed A5 magazine stapled together and sold by burly
men in donkey jackets who resembled Socialist Worker sales-
men, revelled in the absurdity of football supporting, presenting
Darlington's seemingly (and in fact literally) endless difficulties

as a source of bitter comedy. Their columns would evoke leftfield post-punk music such as Joy Division, The Fall, Half Man, Half Biscuit and other bands who had engaged head-on with the grimness of Britain's industrial life, finding ways of turning it into an avant-garde aesthetic which drew on the surrealism, irony and wordplay of terrace culture. They'd also make allusions to writers like Joyce, Beckett and Kafka, a trio who I had, at the time, either not read or was only passingly familiar with. They weren't telling me that watching Darlington was like reading *Endgame* or *The Castle*: they were telling me that I could get to grips with *Endgame* or *The Castle* by using my experiences of watching Darlington.

# Herne Bay 1 – Dulwich Hamlet 3

## 20 APRIL 2013

In 2011, I moved to London with my partner, who had been offered a new job. I had been teaching and lecturing in Norwich, but the precariousness of employment in Britain's higher-education institutions had caught up with me, and that work had disappeared. Working on a further-education course and doing a little ghostwriting, including some in the football industry, gave me an income of sorts, but it made sense to get out of East Anglia. However, after a year and a half in Camberwell, my prospects had not improved substantially: I'd picked up several hourly-paid teaching jobs on the South Coast, and had even given a handful of lectures, but salaried employment was unforthcoming and the energetic and financial cost of the travelling was draining. Life was a grind. I didn't sleep much but, when I managed to drop off, I'd awake soon after and lie for hours, trying to imagine, with little success, how things might be different.

Saturdays had become more important than they'd ever been. Darlington had been demoted to the Northern League, a competition limited to the North East of England, so there was no question of going to watch them regularly given my lack of funds. However, I'd discovered Champion Hill, the ground of Isthmian League Dulwich Hamlet, at the end of my road almost as soon as I arrived in London, and their niche in my affections had widened swiftly. Since the beginning of 2013, I'd started to make friends amongst the small – but palpably growing – group of supporters who gave the otherwise utilitarian stadium its atmosphere, and I'd become a proper home-and-away follower. Come late spring, Hamlet, playing a franchised version of the fashionable Spanish possess-and-press football under progressive manager Gavin Rose, were a few points away from sealing the title of the league's southern division. With Darlington, playing solely in the North East, running away with their league, football at least seemed to be offering some succour.

While there are plenty of easy-come, easy-go clubs participating at the level of the Isthmian South and its equivalents in other parts of the country – some are simply bankrolled village teams, with double-figure attendances – the contest for promotion this season felt properly consequential. In second place, clawing at Dulwich's pink-and-blue shirttails, were Maidstone United, a club who had been in the Football League when I started attending games but had gone bankrupt in 1992. Having reformed and fought their way back through Kent's various county-level leagues, Maidstone had finally returned to a stadium in their home town, and were drawing crowds in excess of 2,000. Dulwich, meanwhile, are a club with pedigree, having won the FA Amateur Cup on four occasions and provided the last non-league player capped by England, the prolific Edgar Kail. Their old ground, adjacent to the present stadium near East Dulwich Station, had hosted a game in the 1948 Olympics: they are a venerated part of the non-league establishment, and a fixture in the memories of the cognoscenti of London football. Located equidistantly between Millwall and Crystal Palace's heartlands, they draw occasional support from fans of both clubs, meaning that their attendances had been healthy for the division even before Rose rejuvenated a struggling team.

On my first few visits to Dulwich, I'd stood alone, watching the game in pleasant metropolitan anonymity with a couple of drinks. One possible course for the club's future seemed obvious. With Palace, Millwall and Charlton all charging excessive admission for walk-up attendees, and with the Brixton, Camberwell and Peckham areas filling up with young, comparatively shallow-pocketed people forced to the capital to seek employment since the 2008 crash, it seemed at least possible that Champion Hill could, gradually, draw attendances in four figures and act as home to a team playing several levels above Step Eight. Indeed, a nascent version of this seemed to be underway even by the time of my first visit. Unlike at most non-league clubs in the UK, there were a number of conspicuously non-local accents to be heard around the pitch – Mancunian, Scots, Scouse – and a preponderance of people in their twenties and thirties who did not resemble the typical customer of an Isthmian League club. Gentrification would be an inaccurate term for what was happening to the club, but there was undeniably a different constituency than would have been found at teams of comparable stature – Sutton, Hampton, Kingstonian, Carshalton – a little further out into the suburbs.

That said, the southern part of the Borough of Southwark and the adjoining sliver of Lambeth have always had a reputation for alterity, with their odd and unmatched combination of ribald cockneyism, bourgeois solidity, genteel artsiness and immigration-driven flux. Angela Carter observed how "London [...] is like Budapest [...] two cities divided by a river" in *Wise Children*, her arch final work from 1991, but Muriel Spark had already struck to the heart of Peckham and Dulwich's otherness, their strange autonomy even within the city-state of London, with 1960's *The Ballad of Peckham Rye*. The Rye, the sprawling, boggy common where a young William Blake had seen "a tree filled with angels, bright angelic wings bespangling every bough like stars" is ten minutes' walk from Champion Hill; Camille Pissarro honed his interpretation of Impressionism a similar distance away on Lordship Lane, tracking the transformation of the area's fields and rolling hills as the railway stretched out the city. In fact, Southwark's political, social and aesthetic separateness could be traced to the late 16th century, when the South Bank served as a pleasure zone for the inhabitants of the more morally hinged city north of the Thames. The Transpontine, as one Dulwich flag declared the area, has been culturally unique for as long as it has existed, and this spirit of almost wilful distinctiveness permeated its local non-league football team to the same degree – but to dissimilar effect – as it had Millwall, where exceptionalism had often been played out in a drama of escalatory machismo.

Over the second half of the 2012–2013 season, Dulwich's away games had turned into a peculiar roadshow, with upwards of a hundred fans arriving in comfortable dormitory-town anti-Southwarks and Kentish seaside resorts, and staging something that blended a semi-facetious parody of European *ultraismo* and the prole art threat of late-Eighties fanzine culture. We were there, in the first instance, to watch the football, but a lot of us were also chattering about left politics, art theory, Detroit techno, the social history of South London – and this wasn't, *contra* to more recent accusations, a case of "hipsters" or "latecomers". Indeed, the surge of support that had come with Rose's management only seemed to bring out a penchant for iconoclasm that was intrinsic to the club, or even to British football in general. When Margaret Thatcher died the day before the League Cup final against Essex side Concord Rangers, it hadn't only, or even predominantly, been new fans or students singing anti-Thatcher songs. Old stagers had been rubbing the footballing authorities up the wrong way almost since Kail's day; now the shifting demographics of the area were acting as a force multiplier for this cussedness.

We were heading to Herne Bay on the north coast of Kent and I was kneeling on my seat, unshowered, unshaven and drinking a can of lager, talking to my friend Robert on the row behind. He was tired: he worked one-week-on-one-week-off nightshifts and had come into his week off the morning before. He should have rested at home before this big day out, but he'd been booked to do a performance-art piece at a Shoreditch gallery the evening before. "Why are you covered in glitter?" asked a Dulwich veteran. "I was out late last night doing interpretative dance", Robert replied, in a suburban drawl even he'd describe as John Lydon done by Janet Street-Porter. No one considered this unusual. We nudged out of the traffic around the Catford Gyratory and headed for the A2, drinking, talking, occasionally singing.

An hour or so later, we arrived outside Herne Bay's piece-meal, picturesque ground to be greeted, to general amusement and sarcasm, by the sight of a huge Union Jack painted with an Ulster Loyalist slogan. North Kent, over the last ten or so years, has become the lodestone of the British new right's grievances: nearby Thanet, with its respectively faded and eviscerated resorts of Margate and Ramsgate, was an area of strategic importance for the anti-European, anti-immigrant populism of the United Kingdom Independence Party. Like Barrow, the littoral of South-Eastern England feels like it has not caught up with the 21st century, but in some regards, one might argue, this makes it abso-lutely emblematic of the same period, an era in which the future seems to have failed and all that is available appears to be various species of nostalgia and symbolic irredentism. We were a short sixty miles from South London, but little seemed to have shifted in Herne Bay, save the technology in the arcades on the front, since the 1990s. What set it apart from a place like Barrow was the object of its bygones: where the Cumbrian town staged the twi-light of British industry, Herne Bay evoked the vanished leisure of the Southern English working class, the day-outers from London for whom Brighton or Margate would have proved a bit much.

We wandered into town for a drink, about thirty of us taking over a pub which was empty apart from one old man who, either coincidentally or fictionally, turned out to have played for Dul-wich in the 1950s. No one could recall hearing his name before, but non-league football can be like that, and certainly was in the postwar years: assuming your circle of acquaintance is not limit-ed to merchant bankers and minor aristocrats, the chances are you know several people who have played senior (as opposed to Sunday) football. It's hardly a mark of note or distinction. At university alone, I had several friends who had played in the opening rounds of the FA Cup, turning out in front of thirty or forty people on baking August days with the theoretical possibility of Wembley as one incentive alongside the slightly more realistic one of getting through a few rounds and drawing a bigger club.

This aspect of British football is the bit most people seem to misapprehend, completely regardless of the manifest evidence. The infrastructure of the senior game not only in England, but in Scotland and Wales, constitutes a huge sprawl of clubs – well over a thousand, in fact – who fit into neither the paradigms of professionalism nor of park football. Non-league is routinely dismissed by people who watch professional clubs as "one man and his dog" watching a game on "a roped-off park pitch": it is anything but. These are clubs with floodlights, stands, supporters' clubs, safety licences, Inland Revenue bills, travelling costs and playing budgets, clubs that exist in often fractious relationships with the general economy and whose playing staff exist in a fractious relationship with the professional game. Even at a level lower than that of Dulwich and Herne Bay, the worst insult you can aim at someone on the books of a senior club is that they are a "park player". Their routes into the liminal space between the professional and the properly amateur games vary wildly, with some dropping out of the academy systems of league clubs, some having chosen to proceed with academic studies, some earning more outside football than they could by devoting themselves to it, and some (particularly in the South of England) trying to make a name for themselves after arriving from abroad, sometimes as refugees. What unites them is the intuitive knowledge that this is more than a game for them, more than simple recreation.

This is an attitude which reflects onto the fans of non-league clubs. Again, nothing antagonises them more quickly than the idea that what they do is somehow deviant, but they do enjoy, to some extent, the kudos of marginality. For some – and perhaps I'm one of them, for my sins – that taps into a broader interest in the non-mainstream, something that might also be expressed as an interest in alternative music, independent cinema, cult literature or even real ale. For others, non-league is a source of pleasure because of the opportunities it offers for collecting and box-ticking: groundhoppers, for example, are fans who attempt to visit as many senior football grounds as possible to get a "tick", hopefully bringing home evidence of their conquest in the form of a programme. This group are the one who frequently earn the opprobrium of fans of "big" football and even of other non-league fans, who feel that they reduce the game to equivalence with other para-acquisitive pursuits, particularly trainspotting. A probable majority of non-league followers, however, make it into their sole dabble in obscurantism, something of whose mild oddness they are aware, defensive about and proud of simultaneously. This for them is not only the same thing as "proper" football, it *is* proper football: affordable, socially rewarding, organised without being irredeemably commercialised and, most importantly, executed on occasion by players who, despite being deemed for various rea-sons unsuitable for the professional game, are absolutely brilliant.

In autumn 2012 one of these individuals had found his way to Champion Hill. To date, the 5'2" or 5'3" Anglo-Turkish forward Erhun Oztumer, now a full-time professional with Peterborough but then almost completely unknown, remains one of the two or three players to have given me most pleasure in my spec-tating life. Over the course of the season, Oztumer had scored spectacular goals at an incredible rate: a dead-eyed thirty-yard drive against Folkestone, a briskly executed daisy-cutting volley against Leatherhead, one against Ramsgate that I was too drunk on the day to recall later but has nevertheless come to symbolise the overcoming of footballing impossibility in my mind. He also provided a reliable number of assists with weighted through-balls and telepathic, sharp-angled cutbacks. On their own, however, these things made him merely a fantastically useful player to have on the team: what separated him from effectively and predictably excellent players was his capacity for warping the boundary between the utilitarian and the cosmetic. He ran at defenders clutching the end of his too-long sleeves between his fingers, the perpetual precocious schoolboy even at twenty-two, but his methods of ruining those defenders' confidence were diverse. He'd walk on the ball, step over it, dummy it; suddenly there would be a pristine lawn of space onto which he'd gallop with a level of enthusiasm and commitment not usually associated with number 10s, players often synonymous with lazy mercuriality.

You could never be sure whether or not the tricksiness was inherent to his mission, but it would come about so quickly, and it was so obviously instinctive, that you could be certain that it wasn't part of a calculated strategy of self-aggrandisement. One video of him in a game from that season – against Sittingbourne, attended by fifty or sixty stoned anarcho-punks from German club Altona '93, with whom Dulwich have a fan friendship – encapsulates this. The ball is loose close to the touchline with a Sittingbourne defender anticipating taking possession until Oztumer arrives in the nick of time. You would then expect him to turn the ball back infield, a move that in itself would have required a considerable amount of brio; however, he scoops the ball high over his opponent's head with his trailing left foot, putting the exact amount of spin and pace on it for it to bounce back up onto his chest as he scurries round to collect it, keeping his eye on the target the whole time. A colleague stands out of the way to let him retake possession: the camera is close enough to see the look of disbelief on his face. The marvel isn't located in the technique alone, but in how self-contained the player is while carrying the move out, giving the impression that he's playing entirely in his head and to his own rule-set. It's narcissistic in the sense that Freud implies when he describes narcissism as the charm of inscrutability possessed by small children and cats: not vain, but something which suggests that whatever is taking place in the object of observation's head is fascinating, and that we're never going to get to know about it.

At Herne Bay, however, Oztumer was not in the starting eleven. Dulwich had lost a bruising match with Leatherhead earlier in the week and their star player had come in for some special attention from the Surrey club's looming defenders. It had long been anticipated that Rose would rest him, and here was the occasion, despite it being a game that had become imperative to win. Only one team wins automatic promotion from the southern division of the Isthmian League: those in the second to fourth positions must play-off for the remaining spot, and Dulwich had lost consecutive play-off finals at Leatherhead and Bognor. Herne Bay had tumbled down the league in the second part of the season, and had just fired their manager, but I remembered their visit to Champion Hill in autumn as an afternoon when our victory had been a very close one earned in the last ten minutes of the game. As the match kicked off and we occupied the stand behind the goal, a brick construction with the air of an unfinished domestic garage, we were clearly nervous and distracting ourselves by watching trains pass on the mainline which ran behind the stand to our right. With the pre-game drinking and the lucidity of the late spring day, the game and the world beyond it felt far-off and untouchable without being exactly irrelevant, near enough to be a source of anxiety but too distant to intervene in.

This is one of two cardinal experiences of watching football you have any investment in, and it makes most sense when explained in the light of its opposite. On occasion, it appears that the crowd have an agency which is comparable to, if not greater than, that of the players, and that you can somehow will the ball to be where you want it to be. Players tend to claim that the crowd does act as an inspiring or motivating force, although I've never been quite sure whether or not this is true or just thoughtful lip-service. After all, as I've just pointed out, some of the very best moments of footballing acumen I've been party to have seemed to involve a player locking out totally any context whatsoever and operating entirely in their head, albeit with a manifest physical consequence. There is little hard evidence bar player anecdote that your energy as a supporter contributes particularly to what the footballers are doing, at least in the immediate sense of how they use the ball in a particular move. Nevertheless, supporters frequently behave as if this is the case. But this form of commitment exists in tandem with a *glazed* watching of the game, where the fans have no influence whatsoever over the outcome of the game and the action might as well be happening on television. Indeed, on-pitch events can bring on an experience akin to dissociation, particularly in the uncanny silence that follows a goal for the opposing team, before the noise from the other end of the pitch reaches you. One's relationship with the outside world becomes queasy and vertiginous, desperate for some form of pinching confirmation.

Fortunately, this came ten minutes into the game. Dulwich's winger broke through in the channel and scuffed a left-footed shot which kicked back off the hard, bumpy pitch, evading the Herne Bay goalkeeper at his far post. Warm lager arced through the air. With only two home games against relatively poor teams to go after this, we could feel the title, nearly ours, and start thinking about next season's adventures. The rest of the half was uneventful: without Oztumer, we created few chances, but our opponents had little to threaten us with. For the uninitiated, non-league can be like this: you see some teams who are decently well-organised and competent enough to stop you from scoring, but will never find a goal of their own unless there's a severe lapse in concentration from their opponents. In my experience, managers at this level of football are prone to over-concentration on one particular aspect of the team, meaning that high scorers are unlikely to defend particularly well and vice-versa. This lack of balance is, technically, a weakness of the non-league game and can lead to some tedious matches, although it also means that some teams who are in theory very good can occasionally collapse shockingly against teams who are in theory very bad. It also explains to some degree just how fine the margins are at this level: one player can have a level of impact in the semi-professional game in a way the professionals would be unlikely to recognise.

After a halftime spent in the bar, which meant that we were now, for the most part, incredibly drunk indeed, we found our way into an even odder terrace, which had brick partitions running down it like seaside groynes, for the second half. Upon winning a free kick twenty-five yards from goal, Rose decided that the time had come to introduce Oztumer, who was greeted with an ululating chant we'd learned from his cousins and their friends, London-based Galatasaray fans who occasionally turned up to watch Hamlet with flares, drums and banners. He immediately ran over to the dead ball; there was no question about who was going to strike it. Seconds later, the ball was in the roof of the net and various friends were grabbing me and kissing me, beerily and hairily, on the lips. A bottle of vodka was produced. Then Herne Bay scored, Dulwich immediately restored their two-goal lead, and the second half ended as abruptly as the first had dragged. We were four points, we calculated, from the title. After the game, it was back, once again, to the bar, where about twenty of us surrounded our French full-back and sang, or at least loudly hummed, the Marseillaise at him.

The best portrayal of a South London accent in fiction came from the bleak crime novelist Derek Raymond, who described a policeman whose voice "gutter[s] in his throat like a flame in a cracked chimney". It's a manner of speaking with a certain level of aggressive presence, a measured and sceptical tone which splinters or peels away from itself under the exertion of articulating joy. No other English regional accent is so guarded in its middle ranges. The coach back to Dulwich, then, was a rare chance to hear that voice at the limits of its expressivity: to hear, in fact, the sound South London makes when things have, beyond any reasonable doubt, worked out well. That sound is a kind of voiced silence, a way of filling the air after a phrase like "it was". "It was", followed by a not-really-empty emptiness, a charged gap in speech. We'd run out of drink and even of water, and the early evening sun was cooking us in a long line of traffic caused by what we'd heard was a quite bad accident ahead of us on the A2, but the fact everyone seemed to have run out of anything to say was evidence of how promotion was only a few points away. We arrived back in London around eight: I went home and straight to bed, back into the folds of malaise, and wished that I could sleep until Tuesday night.

CHAPTER TWO

# Players

We were treated like pieces of meat.
– Various footballers, *in conversation and interview*

There was a point about four or five years ago, a point I'm not bothered about confirming archivally but which nonetheless definitely occurred, at which football clubs almost uniformly, if you'll allow the pun, changed the way that they marketed their new kits. Not so long ago, you'd have found a posed shot of a star player rehearsing some fabulous piece of technique or even, where the club had a meagre branding budget, a simple team photograph which could create other revenue streams from calendars and similar items. What superseded these more traditional forms of marketing was a style of image which offers the contemporary student of semiotics much to consider. Now, the background will be an electrolysed *Blade Runner* gloom, perhaps with little serifs of smoke indicating some recent conflagration or catastrophe. Against this will stand three to five players, one of whom will be a goalkeeper, another a winger or attacking midfielder, and yet another a looming centre-half with a backwoodsman's beard and sleeve tattoos. Their arms are crossed and resolute; they are indomitable. The language used to sell the kits will be pared down to abstraction: "[Club Name] 2015 Home Kit: We Are One." The general tone is a seriousness so ascetic it detonates into camp, unable to withstand the internal stresses on its structure of plausibility.

Nevertheless, for some it *must* have the appeal of gravitas or it would simply not work as an incentive to purchase. How, then, can it be explained? First, perhaps, with recourse to a certain type of pop-cultural hetero-masculinity which (re-)emerged in the early 21st century, initially – if I had to pick a particular moment – with the success of Peter Jackson's *Lord of the Rings* adaptations, but more lately underwritten and refocused with HBO's preternaturally successful *Game of Thrones*. In these programmes' fantasy second worlds, manhood, if done properly and honourably, is a matter of disenchanted seriousness, a saddened and reluctant understanding of the inherently conflictual nature of existence. Any levity here can only manifest itself as grim irony – one does not simply walk into Mordor, remember – and all time between battles must be occupied with sorrowful renditions of stories of the travails of Good. The bearded, tattooed centre-half on the kit advert, then, is supposed to connote the fantasy version of ordeal, the effect of which is not limited to football's contemporary image-system. Think, for example, of how car advertising has departed from its Nineties staple of secure glamour to its present mood of quasi-military exertion, its stubbled protagonists surging through sodden Scandinavian or Scottish gloom in order not, as the case would once have been, to seduce, but to be reunited with family.

The last item in this chain of images is, of course, the military-recruitment film, which has become, after a fashion, more honest and explicit about the danger and brutality of conflict in the period that I'm describing. In Britain, the army are no longer particularly reticent about depicting "live" skirmishes in their propaganda, in part because they suspect that computer games are not far from offering a comparable intensity of experience anyway, but also because of a gathering idea which automatically associates soldiering with virtuousness. Ideally, the film prompting its audience to enlist in the Marines or for the Territorial Army shows a gunfight in Helmand, or on a generically be-jungled

"African" coastline populated by similarly generic "rebels", before portraying the hero returning to the family that his actions have (somehow) safeguarded.

What I'm trying to get at here is how advertising aimed at men has undergone an elemental shift in how it desires, and in how it seeks to channel desire. The old, but not really that old, male utopia was one of ease, of frictionless libido cruising through a collage of Eurocentric sophistication, waking in Venice amidst the accoutrements of one erotic encounter and falling asleep in Monte Carlo amidst another's. This no longer holds: it is perceived, understandably, as inauthentic and insufficiently austere for our times. Instead, the dream-work is of extended periods of sexual and romantic isolation in the still largely homosocial realms of military conflict or extreme exploration, interspersed with brief unifications with family. This is the logic to which football advertising in Britain increasingly appeals.

Clearly, nobody seriously thinks that the players of, say, Scunthorpe United visiting, say, Leyton Orient for an awayday is remotely comparable to a six-month tour of Helmand. Nevertheless, enough sticks from this metaphorical equivalence to make us think that footballers fulfil some kind of existential duty, something which exceeds the rubric of paid work, when they play for a team. It has long been the case that disloyalty has been the most atrocious crime a footballer can commit, but the economic insecurity of the historical moment seems to have amplified the notion that we have particular responsibilities to increasingly local social units. There is something especially interesting here in the way that football clubs now seem to be regarded as ends in themselves on this front, as entities more demanding and deserving of loyalty than the broad communities which they inhabit.

One concrete example of the contrasting fortunes of club and community is Liverpool fans' relative silence over the acts of social cleansing allegedly committed in the vicinity of Anfield.

In the streets surrounding the Reds' ground, houses have supposedly been bought on behalf of the club; these houses are then boarded up, suppressing property and land value in the area, thus driving down the cost of any future stadium expansion. The lack of major outcry about this suggests that – to slip into modern managerial rhetoric for a moment – This Football Club is regarded as something that fans regard as a rallying point for social allegiance which supersedes the needs of its immediate environment. As I've said above, the club becomes an end in itself, and the player, correspondingly, must behave as an avatar of the club's struggle in an increasingly atomised, conflictual world. They must buy wholesale into the "values" and "philosophy" of the "project", even when "project", "philosophy" and "values" are mere *ad hoc* conjurings of recently installed owners and managers whose heads have been turned by the jargon of "smart-thinking" books and TED talks.

"Sport is a battle", then, is the metaphor we are now required to live by as football fans. The club must survive and prosper at the cost of everything else. However, this formula changes somewhat in international football, where the "need" for victory is often sutured unquestioningly to the national cause. Curiously, this relationship seems to intensify even as the sense of common purpose between clubs and communities fades. This came to light in a peculiarly candid way during the predictable period of recrimination following England's equally predictable early exit from the 2014 Brazil World Cup. Even before the players had set off for home Harry Redknapp, the geezerish and journalist-friendly cockney who had been passed over for the England manager's job in 2012 because of a pending court case, turned up in the press claiming that a number of English internationals were in the habit of begging their club managers to withdraw them from the national squad for friendly games. The allegation was stark: that some English players regard playing for their country not as an honour, but as an annoyance. England coach Roy Hodgson and his outgoing captain Steven Gerrard cannily took the sting out of Redknapp's comments by asking him to name names, but the matter did not drop entirely. Former England striker and current light-entertainment go-to Ian Wright wrote in his column in the *Sun* newspaper that any player found to have shirked international "duty" without good reason should be required to phone the parents of a soldier killed in Afghanistan to explain their decision to drop out.

This was imagined on Twitter in plenty of bleakly funny versions of how the transcript of such a call might read. Palpably, the suggestion was a piece of attention-seeking on the part of Wright, who has never, it seems, got over his early-career rejections or his marginalisation in the 1990s England team by more rounded strikers such as Alan Shearer. However, it spoke to something in England's present-day ideological make-up, namely a resurgent patriotism of symbols which regards Englishness, whatever that might mean, as somehow under threat. The role the football player takes in this set of beliefs is intriguing. Wright was playing to the idea that the default setting for footballers is a patriotic one, that they feel a sense of pride in national symbols which extends beyond their utilitarian, team-bonding value. By linking this version of patriotic obligation to that of the soldier's, he tacitly insists on the relative unanimity of nationalistic sentiment amongst the working-class communities that both footballers and the rank-and-file military are drawn from.

While one does find the occasional player, such as Serbia's Siniša Mihajlović or Croatia's Zvonimir Boban, for whom patriotism is obviously a very real and visceral thing, it seems plausible and even likely that the average international player uses it as a motivational tool, a way of rationalising responsibility to the footballing cause. There's a ludicrous misrecognition on the part of the right-wingers doing their Queen-and-country act in the stands who think the men on the pitch automatically share their blood-and-soil mentality: footballers, like most sportspeople, tend to focus themselves out of any formal political identification and even, in some cases, vaguer political affects. Presenting footballers as exclusively patriotically motivated is a form of fantasy about working-class politics, which is to say that it suits certain agendas to treat the "proles" as intrinsically nationalistic, thus implicitly turning anti-nationalistic (typically socialist) politics into an illegitimate bourgeois charade. And here lies the true equivalence between footballers and soldiers. The majority join the military because of the route it offers out of poverty, regardless of the narrative which states that they do so through an unmediated love of the *patria*. This narrative has, both in the UK and the US, a double function, simultaneously masking socio-economic inequality and lending affective "credibility" to those countries' ridiculous joint-enterprise neo-imperial wars. The linking of footballers to soldiers, then, has as its ultimate outcome an intensification of the militarisation of British society, the same phenomenon, in fact, that we witness when, on the occasions when England score a goal at an international tournament, the footage cuts away to show soldiers watching the game from whichever theatre of operations they have been sent to in the latest stage of the quixotic War on Terror.

That said, the determinations of an intensified seriousness in the visual language of the football media are not limited to society's broader militarisation. One thinks of the way that various England internationals from the present and the recent past, such as the aforementioned Gerrard, John Terry and new captain Wayne Rooney, seek to present themselves to the nation. The media consensus around the England team emphasises their surfeit of passion, which supposedly exists in inverse proportion to a shortfall of technical ability and tactical nous, but to actually watch an England game is, very often, to be struck by the cowed performances and expressions of players we are supposed to think of as possessed of leonine bravery and aggression. These are rarely performances full of sound and fury but lacking in signification: in fact, they are bereft of *all* these attributes.

Gerrard is perhaps most representative of how a reputation for passion accrues around a player who does not always display it, or seems to exude its mere facsimile. There is still available online a video which shows the erstwhile Liverpool and England captain comforting his then team-mate Luis Suarez after Liverpool had relinquished their claim to the Premier League title in 2014 with a frenetic 3–3 draw at Crystal Palace. As Suarez pulls his jersey up to dry his tears, Gerrard shoos away a television camera attempting to capture the Uruguayan's despair. Or does he? The image captures the quintessence of Gerrard, by which he is simultaneously an outstanding captain, a leader and motivator *par excellence* genuinely concerned for his charges, and a simulacrum of that thing. As he wards away the camera, it seems also as if he's soliciting it. Protecting Suarez from the intrusive glare of the media is clearly the responsible thing for a captain to do, and one's immediate response here is to think that the act denotes some fundamental decency. However, the suspicion gradually emerges that what is really happening is that he is comprehensively aware of the power of such an image, and *that he needs to be seen not wanting to be seen*.

Gerrard's career is almost precisely coterminous with the Blair – Brown – Cameron era in British politics. In this period, the affective aspect of politics has intensified in counterpoint to a more generalised "waning of affect": being seen to "care", or to share in spuriously "common" desires which have replaced genuine collective purpose, seems to be regarded as a far safer bet electorally than possessing either proven competence or the potential for developing it. At the same time, and this is something which takes us once again to those portentous kit advertisements, the tenor of branding has changed significantly, with the governing maxim no longer "this product is great" but "this product is invested with passion". We're passionate about conservatories! We're passionate about crisps! We're passionate about dog food! However much it cloys with us, it is hard to believe in an individual who is not to some extent invested in aspects of these values, for who would want to be perceived as *not caring*?

To be regarded as wrongly or cynically motivated is something which footballers must deal with constantly: no wonder Gerrard, Terry, Rooney and the like must seek not only to play football well, but to come across as adequately invested, when they and the rest of their profession are subject to constant slights about the essential worthlessness of what they do. For all the substantial material recompense playing the sport earns them, there are few jobs which invite more clamorous accusations of social irrelevance and metaphysical inanity. This is an issue which comes up every time there is a big international competition. Of course, football becomes unpleasantly ubiquitous during the World Cup, with the main sufferer of this ubiquity being not those who don't enjoy the game but, counterintuitively, those who do. The unpleasantness is a consequence of ubiquity's tendency towards dilution, which has the consequence of football being turned into "footie", that abstracted version which lends itself to all kinds of dismal exercises in masculinist and nationalistic identity formation. Watch the footie on telly last night, *mate*? Well, no, I *went to the football* last night. If you spend every weekend of the season following a team, it is pretty easy to come to feel alienated during the World Cup or European Championships, when the sport becomes the preserve of geezerish dilettantes and the themed ladvertising kicks in. It's at this stage that I usually start to feel sympathy for people who dislike football entirely.

That's until things turn up like the irritating 2014 meme imagining an alternate reality in which archaeology, rather than football, dominates the media and archaeologists are paid thousands of pounds a week. In the weeks leading up to the World Cup in Brazil, this became the definitive plaint on the behalf of the non-believers, the document tasked with articulating to football fans just what it means to be on the outside of the festivities. Despite the fact that I can imagine what it must be like, for the precise reason that I largely *feel the same*, for the non-football fan to be bombarded with "footie" for a whole month every second summer, I couldn't identify at all with the meme:

> Even when it isn't archaeology season, the media follow noted archaeologists. They drive fast cars, date beautiful women, advertise fragrances, and sometimes they go to nightclubs and act in the worst possible way. Scandals erupt as the tabloids follow these new celebrities when they're not searching the world for answers.

Something like this emerges on the Internet every time there's an international tournament, but rarely has the argument come so heavily macerated in *bêtise*. Hiding behind a curtain of liberal affability and an admittedly adept deployment of an affectation of evenhandedness, this is a piece of writing which rests upon a set of assumptions about football, and particularly about football fans and players, which are ideological.

Let's think, first of all, about why it is specifically archaeology which replaces football in this ostensibly harmless thought experiment. Why not, say, "shopping" or "military history"? I have no score to settle with archaeology – who would, honestly? – and appreciate the discipline's substantial, if not politically unproblematic, contribution to the sum total of human self-understanding. However, the field does have certain connotations which are useful in particular forms of self-presentation. Archaeology carries with it an image of wistful past-gazing, of laudable knowledge-foraging, of being the kid who ignored football in the playground because they were too busy digging away in the corner looking for clay pipes or Neolithic man. For all of its fascinations, it is also a realm in which the humblebragging, self-anointed geek enjoys considerable social capital.

In other words, it's just the kind of thing which appeals to that online constituency Jacques Lacan anticipated when he said that thing about how *les non-dupes errent*, how the non-dupes are mistaken. That it is the not-fooled, the people who "see through stuff", who are the most taken-in ideologically, has always had a considerable degree of appeal, but never more so than in the era of internet atheism, an age in which meme factories like the smug I Fucking Love Science pour out quotable rationalism seemingly by the second. *Lovely* archaeology coming on as a substitute for aggressive, alpha-male, avaricious, irrational (and, though the piece would never dare mention it, largely working-class) football seems to me the kind of notion that really speaks to the aren't-bees-more-fascinating-than-Jesus, calling-Valentine's-Day-Hallmark-Holiday, Stop-Kony crowd.

But, lest we fail Practical Criticism 101, let's go back to the text itself. The point of the meme, remember, is to induce some sort of artificial parity between football and archaeology – to ask us to imagine if archaeology, presented without additional ideological freight, and football, presented likewise, swapped places in the cultural imagination. However, the writer cannot resist the opportunity to start introducing other elements into the equation almost as soon as it has been established, finding subtle ways of embedding value judgements. Here, it's imagined that archaeologists acquire the same, "worst possible" behavioural traits that the media at large attributes, with consummate dishonesty, to *all* footballers. The rationale for doing this is not, as it purports to be, to get us to imagine archaeologists on an alcohol-fuelled rampage in Mayfair, but to remind us that football players are uncouth (working-class) louts who provoke "scandal".

Then there's another dig. Having hypothesised an archaeologist who would "act" like a footballer, the writer reminds
us what an archaeologist would be doing when they're not up
to no good, namely "searching the past for answers". That's to
say that their professional activity would still be of considerable value, inviting a comparison to the implied "pointlessness"
of football. Such purported pointlessness is a classic canard of
a hypocritical utilitarianism which locates value (or "point") in,
say, BBC4 documentaries about archaeology or Scandinavian
crime dramas, but not in competitive sport. This, I suspect, is
an aspect of that classic piece of political equivocation by which
utilitarianism is good for the working-class goose, but not
appropriate for the middle-class gander, one which seems to be
reserved largely for football.

The reason for examining this apparently frivolous meme
– which is itself an attempt to dismiss football as frivolous – in
so much detail is to think through the latent assumptions people have about not only the fans, but the players, of the game,
something which might help us to understand the verbal and
visual rhetorics of passion and authenticity which have become
increasingly common in the last decade. Why is it that players
(and managers) feel the need to justify themselves with reference
to a discourse of ordeal? Well, it would seem to be a lazy middle-
class dismissal of the supposed fetishism of football, which is, in
turn, a fetishisation of not-football, of a nebulously demarcated
space of "culture" and "the arts", of all the modes of commodi-
fiable liberal pseudocynicism from the depressingly ubiquitous
media presence of alt-comedy to geek culture's stylised war on
both intellectual "pretension" and sporting "stupidity". This not-
really-sceptical scepticism, which dismisses both "high" and "low"
culture as somehow inauthentic, and which binds the near-right
and the near-left together in British media culture, works at a
level of constant invalidation. What happens, then, when they

encounter a figure who seems to want to put a foot in the "low" and the "high" while passing over their middle?

Queen's Park Rangers midfielder Joey Barton provoked a storm of think-pieces, and their derivative online chaff, in 2013 when it was announced that he was going to study for a philosophy degree. The tough-tackling and frequently controversial Liverpudlian had already become something of a figure of fun over the preceding couple of years because of his Twitter feed, on which he had not been shy to quote a number of well-known thinkers, with favourites including Oscar Wilde, Nietzsche and Orwell. However, his revelation that he was going to Roehampton University – "eyes peeled, ears open, brain engaged" – provoked a minor outrage. What, the press wondered, could a footballer hope to bring to a philosophy classroom? The discussion was entirely predictable: the big newspapers made jokes about the unlikeliness of the situation and puns around the "brains in their feet" trope, while a few contrarians on the left and right pointed out that this was all snobbery.

However, there was a position that nobody really took into account. Barton's reduction of philosophy to Twitter soundbites, I suspect, offended the middle-class media not only, and probably not even particularly, because they felt philosophy was their "property", but because he inadvertently exposed the embarrassing fact that Britain's culture of public intellectualism, such as it is, operates largely at the level of the decontextualised apercu. Barton quoting well-known Nietzscheanisms felt like a provocative parody of a media class who affect intelligence but have to dismiss any form of critical rigour as "pretension": let's not forget that this is a country in which one of the most common bourgeois dismissals of an idea is that it "belongs in Pseuds' Corner". It's okay to be Stephen Fry, with his chummy, witty, empirical fact-sowing, but to aspire to develop a knack for quotation into any kind of analytical elegance is to forget the rules of the game.

What scared the broadsheets about Barton was not the threat of a working-class footballer matching their cultural capital, because in effect he had *already done so* merely by knowing how to quote Nietzsche. The real fear was that he might start to transform dilettantism into critical power.

The other interesting aspect of Barton's presentation as "football's philosopher king", as David Dimbleby introduced him on a particularly fractious episode of *Question Time*, is how his often-ridiculed ideas are so commensurate with a generalised tendency in British, or more particularly English, thought. Reading his Twitter feed is to go through a series of contradictions between anti-establishment grizzle, a deep-rooted dislike of hierarchical authority, and the individualistic snarling which manifests itself most damagingly in politics as populist Toryism. Barton seems to have little time for the wealthy and the historically powerful, but he's also anti-statist, anti-taxes, pro-"hard work" and "pulling yourself up" – values he shares with a number of other players. This is an attitude which presents itself as rebellion, and its antecedents would include Fifties realist novelists such as Alan Sillitoe and working-class musicians from John Lennon to Noel Gallagher and beyond, but it has always proved itself fully absorbable by the establishment. Again, the annoyance people seem to experience because of Barton might be read as little more than a confused hostility to an ideology to which they themselves subscribe.

What of other so-called "footballing intellectuals"? Sometimes, a player needs to do little more than read the *Guardian* and visit the cinema, like the former Blackburn and England full-back Graeme le Saux, to earn this title. Others have had their tastes more clearly pinned down, such as the former Scottish international winger Pat Nevin, who writes frequent columns on culture for newspapers and was once invited on *Newsnight* to discuss James Joyce's play *Exiles*. Then, of course, there's Eric Cantona, a player who seemed genuinely capable of effecting a seamless continuity between the grace and volatility of his off-field interests – symbolist poetry and expressionist painting – and his style of play on it. Nevertheless, however much one might celebrate these figures for their apparent determination to go against the grain of their profession, there's an argument to be made that they manifest yet one more instance of our strange demand that footballers exhibit something above and beyond their fulfillment of the immediate terms of their contract. The acclamation of the Cantonas and Nevins is the flip-side of the tendency that demands that passion is shown, because it still demands that the game of football generates a meaning beyond itself to match (and thereby, perhaps, rationalise) the obsessive meanings generated by *fans* of football.

Perhaps, though, the more intriguing story about football players concerns neither their function-transcending passion for the game, and for the club they play the game for, nor their capacity for intellectual and political commitments which elicit patronising surprise. Talk to a professional player, even one who has had a financially successful career, and you'll often find a measure of resentment about the way that they were abstracted into the sport's labour market in the first place. In the not-too-distant past, it was common for British clubs to discourage developing talents from concentrating on their academic studies, with the result that a player who failed to make the much-mythologised "grade" could find themselves without qualifications or skills at an age when his peers were starting work or university. The other outcome of this is that players finishing a career approach a very real wilderness: if they do not want to stay within football in some way, usually coaching, they have to make a new place for themselves in the world, a task which often proves to be extremely challenging ("Why would I want to go to university when I'll be fifteen years older than everyone else – I'd just look stupid", as one said to me). To commit to the sport as a career is a risk which pays off, in as much as it actually manages to provide a "career" worthy of the name, for a minority, and it is a minority of that minority who make the fathomless riches players are supposed to make. It is a precarious lifestyle, and becoming more so.

About eighteen months ago, I realised that, with a game the following morning, the toe of my boots had split open and I needed to replace them. I went down to the pile-high-sell-cheap sports shop in Peckham, staffed by zero-hour workers, and found myself sitting on the chair trying on a pair of cheap boots next to a young man from Central Africa who was in the process of buying the same item. He was paying considerably more attention to the technical features of his new footwear than I was, and the reason became clear when his phone rang and he answered it: his agent was calling, to discuss a trial he was to have the following week, in Poland. Europe is now home to a number of young players invited from Africa by spurious footballing agencies who then fail to provide jobs on arrival, meaning that football at all levels across the continent has a constant army of reserve labour willing to put in the unpaid work of travelling from place to place, from country to country, from England to France to Cyprus to Ukraine, in the hope of finding a stable contract. Expanding this new sporting precariat is a system of academy development in the professional game which oversigns players, meaning that substantial numbers drop out and have to find ways of sustaining themselves financially while they look for a way back into the full-time game or retrain.

Michael Calvin's outstanding book on football scouting in the globalised world, aptly titled *The Nowhere Men*, demonstrates that the sport as we know it is sustained by vast amounts of unremunerated or inadequately remunerated work, carried out not only by players but by volunteer ground staff, catering workers, scouts and, of course, the parents who give up swathes of free time to provide support for children who are trying to make their name.

The other fundamental that his work reveals is that the margin of error for footballing success is minute: that it is the tiny, eminently missable detail, the shape of a body as a pass is intercepted or the way the foot follows through a shot, on which scouts and coaches make decisions. The affective surplus that supporters demand, and are culturally encouraged to demand, from players, can only ever be an addition to an amount of refined playing ability that non-players barely perceive. Nine hundred and ninety times out of a thousand, the worst player in a professional game is incalculably better than the best in an amateur one.

Nevertheless, we are now technologically equipped to register the minutiae of skills which once seemed so intangible to the non-professional. Once, fans had to lock up a great piece of technique in their memories: they went to games hoping that a player could provide what Johnson's narrator in *The Unfortunates* calls "that one moment". Subsequently, the moment lost some of its aura as games were recorded, with season highlights being made available for purchase on video. One had an increased chance of being able to watch a piece of technique replayed, to try and establish just how the seemingly impossible was executed. Now, we've entered a third stage in which YouTube and Vine reduce football purely to moments of technique, and players to the sum of their detemporalised technical coups. The attention we can commit, as spectators of an infinitely replayed moment, is oddly bifurcated. On one hand, it allows us to understand the physical sequence of an individual move in precise detail, and thereby to think as a connoisseur about the component elements of an individual player's "style". On the other, it causes us to fixate on the distance between us and the professionals, coming eventually to the conclusion that we can't reverse-engineer this artistry in the park. Simultaneously, we appreciate not only how something is done, but also the abject unfeasibility of its being done by us.

While the skills videos assembled on YouTube should hold

enough spectacle in their visual detail to keep us looking, they are invariably soundtracked with maximalist, genre-skipping, super-saturated commercial dance, the virtually inescapable music of affective overload. This returns us, I think, to the militarised images currently used to sell kits. Skill, even when represented with almost pornographic explicitness, and divested of all the tedious cladding of the match, is still not sufficient. Football reduced purely to moments of brilliance continues for some reason to demand narrative, surplus meaning imposed to corroborate with what Lacan calls the Imaginary, that part of the interior life associated with unity and purpose. Competitive structure seems to point in this direction but, as I have already shown, it also innately does the opposite by wiping the slate clean every time a purpose is achieved. We struggle with the idea that playing football is only, in official terms, a career, and for the significant majority of the sport's protagonists fulfills principally material necessities. We could even say that the real ideological significance of football is not that it serves as a distraction, as a social opiate, but that it fails to properly opiate or distract by letting us believe that it has any intrinsic relationship with political meaning and that it is not absurd. Maybe it is this absurdity that fans must assert a claim to if they are ever to truly possess, or repossess the game.

# Newcastle 0 – Arsenal 1

## 29 DECEMBER 2013

The three-carriage train was standing room only by the time it pulled into Newcastle Central. Arsenal were in town, but the passengers boarding from North Yorkshire onwards were all going to support the home team, who had enjoyed an impressive run of results in the lead-up to Christmas, putting them just outside the top four. For Newcastle, it was the season's biggest game so far, an encounter which would set them against the club who had made the early running for the Premier League title. My stepfather, in one of those strokes of luck that seem to happen to people in the building trade, had been offered the loan of two season tickets by a couple of friends, and he'd invited me to come and step outside my footballing comfort zone for an afternoon.

In the UK, it's still the case that, aside from the pantomime, going to the football is one of the few things you can do in the irregular and formless store-cupboard time between Christmas and New Year if you want to retain a handle on your social being. Otherwise it's just the traces and intimations of that: the use-the-year-up gatherings, the china-clinking visits, the bleary conversations in the supermarket when you nip in to buy milk. As the calendar runs down, people actually seem to become less concerned with clock-time and more willing to embrace or experience a purer kind of duration structured only by shifts in the intensity of inactivity. Sport is one of the few ways in which this is contradicted.

In any given year the period between 26th December and 1st January has a busy sporting schedule, with race meets and rugby padding out the already clotted football fixture list. With the transfer window creaking open, managers point to it as a justification for replenishing their squad. It's also the period used to gauge what should be anticipated for the remainder of the season: teams who have started strongly often show cracks in the festive season, while others seem to be stirred by it. Famously, it's a time for results which counteract the logic of the – perhaps proverbial – form-book, a dangerous little spell in which league leaders might collapse at home against a side in the relegation places, inevitably provoking speculation about how players spend their break (an attendant myth suggests some players judiciously pick when to be booked or sent off, so they'll be suspended and therefore unavailable for selection over Christmas).

So, there is something very particular about football in late December. First, it is an odd patch for results. Second, it falls out of line somewhat with the organisation of work-time. Fans seem to look forward to it for both of these reasons, enjoying both the unpredictability and the sense that, here, football is not a reward for work, a pay-off, but something which stands in excess of a reward and is imbued with a suggestion of the gratuitous.

I certainly felt gratuitous. It was my second game in as many days; I had been in Bishop Auckland, Darlington's temporary home, watching a 2–2 draw with Salford in front of a healthy crowd, for the level, of over a thousand. The cold had got right into me, and I'd strained my vocal cords swearing at the referee as the action intensified towards the end. As such, I wasn't really as sprightly as I would have liked as my stepfather and I disembarked, left the station and headed into the alleys leading away from it for a pre-match drink. I'd been looking forward to the game all Christmas, not least because of the frisson, the invertedly perverse kick, of watching a game at a level where the only thing one can really engage with is the action on the pitch. The social experience, at least the social experience of actually being *at* the match, is so broken at the top level – and at the second, third, fourth and arguably fifth levels – of English football that you can't fail to be anything but that archetype of Eighties and Nineties anti-hooligan discourse, the "normal fan just here to watch the game". But the normal fan has become hyper-normal, over-engaged with "the game" by the freakishly detailed regulation of stadia to the extent that the game becomes, in an almost hallucinatory way, *un*watchable.

What exactly do I mean by this? We are fixed into our seats, channelled through a precise series of choreographed movements – the brief chat with a separately-seated acquaintance in the concourse, the checking of the ticket for the exact gangway and aisle, the apologetic shuffle to the seat – that ask us to submit to the idea that watching "the game" is also to be a disciplined activity. Consequently, we begin to ask ourselves questions about the quality of our own spectatorship: this would also seem to transport some of the doubt over whether one is or is not "a good/true supporter". Suddenly, we're overcome with panic. Sitting up here in the second or third tier, the formations look very simple to us – a 4-4-2 setup there, a more modern 4-2-3-1 setup here. But if I can see them, I must be missing something! The very visibility of tactics tells us that they must be a deception, a ruse, a bluff. What am I failing to understand? Is there a subtlety of movement I must appreciate? As with the best seats in the theatre, my watching has become interrupted by the auditing of my own watching.

That was what I was morbidly fascinated by – I had been looking forward, as it were, to watching myself watching myself watch, a study in third-order spectating. And yet I had done the worst thing possible to prepare for this calculated plunge into footballing alienation by attending a game the day before in which I was properly invested, at a level at which a different degree – or at least a different kind – of surveillance is exerted over supporters. At Bishop Auckland, as a chilly winter afternoon turned into a freezing evening and the low hills of south-west Durham, the coal-mined escarpment of the Pennines, faded into crisp night, fans shifted their vantage points as the game progressed, moving between knots of friends, the tea bar, the raffle stand. Since Darlington had been reformed and triply demoted, a sequence of events which had liberated the club from George Reynolds' pompous, unhomely Arena, fans who had boycotted for over a decade began to come back, with many calling the previous season's victory in the ultra-regional Northern League the most enjoyable season off the pitch for twenty years. True, Bishop Auckland was a place of exile, but it was at least one which reinstated the match as a social experience of genuine weight.

That said, another of the things that most interested me about visiting Newcastle – where I hadn't watched a game since, I think, 2002 – was that, at least as far as I could remember, the club is unique in English football in that the area of the ground continues to produce the same kind of situated sociality as it always did on a matchday. Compared even to clubs like Liverpool, Everton and Tottenham, all thought of as specifically representative of their areas, Newcastle are representative of the whole bearing of a place. The ground, St James' Park, is high on a bluff overlooking the area around the station and the Victorian university quarter, below which is the Quayside and the River Tyne. As such, it is visible throughout the city, and particularly from Gateshead, facing Newcastle across the river – in fact, St James' can even be seen from inside Gateshead FC's not inconsiderable stadium. Inevitably, the result of this is that, along with the Tyne Bridge, the ground has default iconic status, and serves as an emotional fulcrum for the city. It's usually facile to compare stadia to religious architecture but, in Newcastle, St James' seems to spatialise the city around it in exactly the same way as the charismatically looming Norman cathedral in nearby Durham. Moreover, the narrow, high-sided streets leading up the hill funnel the approaching fans so that they resemble a religious procession, and the well-established pubs and cafes in these streets allow fans to meet in traditional points of rendezvous which date back to well before the Premier League's self-anointed Year Zero. As a distributor of civic and social meaning, Newcastle United permeates the city in a way which cannot be said for any other large club in England.

What's interesting about this is that, because the social routines of matchgoing have been better preserved here than elsewhere, there's an even more accentuated divide between supporting and spectating when one actually gets into the ground than at allegedly "plastic" clubs like Chelsea or Milton Keynes Dons. In recent years, this division has been underscored by the matter of the club's ownership. During the 1990s, Newcastle experienced a rare period of success thanks to the backing of Geordie entrepreneur John Hall, a figure who adapted the regionalistic verve and purposefulness of T. Dan Smith for the economic milieu of Thatcherism. The sense of regional difference, and importance, cultivated by Smith became the justification for regenerative retail projects, which culminated in Gateshead having what was for a while the largest shopping mall in the world outside North America. Hall went on to become one of a number of local-boys-made-good who "wanted to put something back" into the place which had, confusingly, been impoverished enough to necessitate their "making good" in the first place: there were several of these in 1990s football, most notably Jack Walker, the steel magnate whose financial largesse delivered the 1995 Premier League title to Blackburn Rovers, his hometown club.

Hall was a regionalist whose control of Newcastle began to provoke civic comparisons with Barcelona, rather than with Brasilia, the model for Smith's brutalist regeneration. While his politics stood in direct opposition to those of the reliably Labour-voting city, he was able to gain endorsement on populist grounds. What followed was shambolic. After Hall's son Douglas and associate Freddie Shepherd took over the running of the club, they were caught in a *News of the World* expose ridiculing the people of Newcastle, making derogatory comments about local women and, more unforgivably in the eyes of many fans, mocking United's support base for the financial fidelity which expressed itself in the continuing purchase of expensive merchandise. This provoked a stir, but nothing like that set off by the acquisition of the club in 2007 by Buckinghamshire-born businessman Mike Ashley. Ashley's tenure has seen the club relegated and promoted once again, an almost arbitrary-seeming sequence of managerial appointments and dismissals, an erratic selling policy, the cutting of links with the local media and, most notoriously, the renaming of St James' after his pile-high-and-sell-cheap retail firm Sports Direct. In the immediate aftermath of his arrival, Ashley put on a blokey, even Falstaffian, show apparently aimed at convincing supporters of the purity of his intentions, buying rounds of drinks in the bars of the Quayside and downing a pint at a match in assiduous disregard of ground regulations. Latterly, he has come to be regarded as one of the most ruthlessly business-minded of football-club owners, motivated by profit rather than, as is the case with the Russian and Middle Eastern oligarchs, the desire to get a foot in the door of the UK's cultural life or find a handy distraction from questionable political links. Nor is he like the American consortiums at Liverpool and Manchester United, who keep their eye on the global potential of the clubs' brands. Instead, Ashley has imposed a transfer policy focused on margins rather than on long-term, or even medium-term, playing success: a highly competent scouting network look to sign young players, often from France, still a relatively obscure buying market for English clubs, and sell them on once a period of peak form has multiplied their value. This seems to be done with the goal of making the club look like a viable financial proposition for an investor willing to pay Ashley over the odds to acquire it.

In this sense, Ashley-era Newcastle United are one of the, if not the singular, most nakedly neoliberal football clubs in the United

Kingdom. Some of his decisions – the renaming of the stadium, the appointment of manifestly ill-suited coaching staff – seem to be taken with the unadulterated objective of aggravating the supporters, of reminding them that the club is not a spiritual institution but just one more thing to be melted into air. In its own way, it is a form of enforced disenchantment which appears radically at odds with his earlier desire to convince the public of his emotional involvement.

Approaching St James', drinking in the pubs along Pink Lane or grabbing something to eat in Stowell Street's Geordie Chinatown, is a way of feeling embedded in a place, of perceiving its whole set of dynamic social interchanges. Entering the ground itself, the space which, in its outward-facing exchanges, orients its locale, is, strangely, to become disembedded. It is a Palace of Oz, Kafka's Castle, a place which organises meaning and belief but transpires to be intrinsically devoid of it. We passed through the dark passageways under the Milburn Stand, named in tribute to "Wor" Jackie Milburn, Newcastle's greatest striker and a Tyneside folk hero. Local fans exchanged abuse with visiting Londoners who were queuing to get into the notorious away section, which is so high above the pitch and recessed into the stand that the players are indistinguishable and the match resembles movements on a radar screen. Arsenal fans have a reputation in England for their reticence, and are frequently thought of as the support which has succumbed most fully to gentrification, probably because of Nick Hornby and the location of Highbury, their old ground, in the epicentre of North London's granola republic of Islington. Traditionally, Newcastle would have been thought of as their notional opposite, with a following composed of workers from the shipyards of North Shields and pitmen from the coal coast of south-eastern Northumberland. Here, though, the supposed bourgeois were giving as good as they were getting, if not better – the fans of the host team looked somewhere between

angry and demoralised, in spite of the optimism that had allegedly been generated by their run up the table.

Our seats were in the Leazes End. At the other end of the pitch
stood the Gallowgate End, where Tony Blair was claimed to have
said he had sat as a youth, watching Milburn, despite the fact the
stand was terraced until the 1990s and Milburn moved on when
Blair was four and living in Australia. This turned out to have been
myth-making on the part of local paper *The Sunday Sun*, much to
the chagrin of Blair's opponents and Sunderland fans, who had
taken the story as evidence of their rivals' capacity for rose-tint-
ed tale-telling, alike. The fact that people were even interested
in the idea that Blair would invent such a "memory" is, nevertheless, evidence of Newcastle's atypical political significance, of
the inherency of the football club in the social life of the region.
It is still completely abnormal in Newcastle for somebody born
or even raised locally to support a geographically distant team,
which is not the case in other English regional capitals like Plym-
outh and Norwich.

Yet Ashley has achieved the unthinkable and evacuated St James'
Park of its unique feeling of political centrality. For many years,
Newcastle have entered the field to Mark Knopfler's syrupy, but
ultimately quite beautiful, instrumental composition from the
soundtrack to the film *Local Hero*. The piece ambles through
minor-key melancholy before finding its feet, building to a driving, keening, elongated crescendo which presses all the musical
buttons for pride, courage and nostalgia. Hearing it play as the
team run out has always been my favourite thing about going to
Newcastle, as the crowd as a whole seem to buy into its mood,
the buzz intensifying until the end of the piece when Knopfler's
guitar gives way to the belting songs of the crowd. Yet something
was lacking, and it was the Arsenal fans above us who were once
again in better voice. In the Leazes, people seemed less confident
and purposeful than they did tetchy. As the game started, it was

easy to see why. Newcastle had been sent out with the primary objective of avoiding defeat, of stifling the Londoners' creativity in midfield and pace on the wings. Indeed, they were fielding only one striker, with the French international midfielder Yohan Cabaye pushed up in support in an imitation of attacking intent. The game was characterised by reserve, with both teams falling into a rhythm of backwards and sideways passing, seemingly reluctant to take risks.

Attacking of the most reckless and cavalier type had become an enshrined part of Newcastle's footballing identity, which on Tyneside also means civic and regional identity, during Keegan's reign in the mid-Nineties. That team had won promotion by devastating opponents on a near-weekly basis, and had persevered, profitably, with a shoot-first mentality in the Premier League. Keegan's tactics seemed almost political, a reflection of a growing attitude in the North East which rejected the idea that the region should defer to the supposed sophistication and nuance of London and the South East. Even Keegan's defenders, such as the stylish Belgian Philippe Albert and the floppy-haired wide-boy John Beresford, were picked because of their offensive abilities, and this commitment to entertainment very nearly brought the title north of the River Tees for the first time since Sunderland's victory in 1936. The city's growing ebullience seemed inextricably bound up with what was happening in the football stadium. Even after Newcastle stopped being a serious challenger for the title, they had, under Bobby Robson, another local hero, maintained the philosophy that football games were best won by concentrating on scoring rather than defending.

Although they're in no sense "my" team, it was sad to see them playing in such an inhibited way, their shackles cast off only once as Moussa Sissoko broke down the right to fashion a chance for his French international teammate Mathieu Debuchy. Both players were exactly the type Newcastle fans were anxious about committing to, knowing that a series of good performances might well see them sold in the transfer window. In the concourse, we paid six pounds for a single hot dog and decided it wasn't worth lining up for a beer. Twenty minutes after the break, another French international, this time Arsenal's Olivier Giroud, stooped to head the ball past Newcastle's keeper and give his side the lead, which they retained until fulltime. Newcastle's fans clamoured for a more attacking approach, but it was not until a five-minute period of injury time that their team really exerted any pressure, with Hatem Ben Arfa, the winger whose exile on the substitute's bench had come to symbolise Newcastle's loss of attacking nerve, narrowly missing an opportunity to equalise.

On the final whistle, nobody was sticking around. We wanted to catch the earliest train back to North Yorkshire, and dashed for the exit, but everybody else seemed to be going in the same direction. All at once, it seemed, the crowd came down the hill, filtering into the alleys off Westgate Street and Gallowgate, back into the bars and cafes, the match itself a forgettable intrusion into what was otherwise a good day's socialising – form without any discernible content. How long can it go on like this? How long can most experiences of top-level football consist, essentially, of spending huge amounts of money to sit, bored, in isolating, anti-social "comfort" to watch games defined predominantly by the caution and pragmatism of the weaker team on the field? At Newcastle, the fans seem trapped in a state of just-about liveable dissatisfaction, a condition which, however glib the analogy sounds, persists into 2015 as England's political mood.

CHAPTER THREE

# Tactocracy, Rationalism, Ontology and the Ends of Football

All his stories take place in the same spaceless space, and all holes are so tightly plugged that one shudders whenever anything is mentioned that does not fit in.

– THEODOR ADORNO, 'Notes on Kafka'

In the previous chapters, I've considered various ways in which football, particularly at the top of the game but not exclusively so, has been made subject to viewing practices and forms of encounter which substantively warp its social meaning. In summary, these might be collected under the broad headings of television, the Internet and the corporatised, commercialised or sanitised – delete or add clichés as you please –"matchday experience". Respectively, these ways of engaging with football lead to the game becoming virtualised, fragmented into individual moments of technique which can be packaged for the connoisseur, and made into a space in which the spectator is supposed to apprehend, and acquiesce to, the end of matchgoing as a truly social event. For a long time, it has occurred to me that these phenomena both cause and are sustained by a way of talking about the game which limits it to *something which happens on the pitch*, and that this limiting finds its echoes in discussions of how to further "improve" football using technology such as goal-line cameras and video refereeing. Broadly, what I want to address here relates to a selective recapitulation of rationalism which might better be viewed as privatisation; this essay will, I hope, offer some notes on how to think, resistingly, about this.

In order to privatise something, it needs to be imbued with a minimum of definability which makes its being distinct from what's around it. The minimum level of definability for a sport can be found in its rules, which set out to contain the game, to keep it identifiable. Earlier on, I discussed how the standardisation of rules had given the game the competitive form it needed in order to become a social currency: now, this containment is central to its de-socialisation. However, while containment depends on the rules, the rules are not entirely fallible and their gaps point towards spaces which present a challenge to acts of privatisation. Let's run, then, through a pair of vignettes depicting moments at which the Rules of the Game have proved inadequate either through their inability to speak to a particular situation or because the particular situation makes them difficult to apply with precision.

On 22 June 1986, Argentina played England in a World Cup quarter-final in Mexico City. A short four years previously, the two nations had been military enemies after the UK sent a task force to reclaim the Falklands/Malvinas in the South Atlantic from Argentinian occupation. The sporting and political stakes were high, and a tense first half ended scoreless, the well-organised English defence holding firm against the probings of Argentina's incomparable playmaker Diego Maradona. Six minutes after the break, Maradona and England's goalkeeper Peter Shilton went up on the outskirts of the penalty area to contest a high ball: the attacking player compensated for his disadvantage in height by reaching up to punch the ball over Shilton and into the goal. The referee failed to spot the offence and allowed the goal, which was followed swiftly by another from Maradona as he beat half the England team on a gliding, seemingly inexorably unfolding run from within his own half. Although England pulled one back, and pressed hard to equalise, Argentina held on to reach the semi-final.

Given that the referee missed the original infringement, how ought this to have been dealt with? It is far too easy to express outrage about "cheating" here, to forget that any individual match anywhere, at any time, will provide, given sufficiently attentive analysis, examples of players *deliberately* breaking the rules following a brief calculation both of their likelihood of being caught, and the punishment they can expect if they are. One argument, of course, is that – as is the case in other sports – an extra official can monitor video footage of the game, having dispensation to halt play to inform the referee of any wrongdoing. But this course of action also proves fallible.

If one winds forward twenty-four years from Maradona's deadlock-breaking punch in the Azteca Stadium, they will find another World Cup quarter-final in which handball played a critical role. However, the incident in question could not have been accounted for had video-refereeing technology been available. In the final moments of extra time as Ghana faced Uruguay in Johannesburg, hoping to become the first African World Cup semi-finalists in the first African-hosted World Cup, the Uruguayan Luis Suarez saved a goalbound shot with his hands. Instead of getting the goal which would have seen them into the last four, Ghana instead had to take a penalty, which Asamoah Gyan missed, hitting the crossbar. The match went to a penalty shoot-out, which the South American side won, although Suarez, sent off for his offence, was banned for the remainder of the competition. Here, a video referee would have made no difference whatsoever, as the rules state clearly how to deal with the situation in question: stop play, show a red card to the offending player, and award a penalty. Yet the rules are, if not completely inadequate, somewhat fragile here, as they allow a defending team to reduce a goal which – if nobody "cheats" – is *certain* into one which is merely statistically *probable* simply by sacrificing a player.

What one realises when faced with such a case is that the Rules of the Game are shadowed by another rule-set which allows a certain amount of calculated transgression to occur and, arguably, reduces the written laws to a code of etiquette, a breakable symbolic register. Football is, of course, *on one hand* a set of comprehensively codified rules about what can and can't be done with the ball by the twenty-two players on the pitch. But this is a limited account, because those rules can't minister to every category of impaired decorum. For the full effect of football to be appreciated, perhaps, we need to think about those moments in which an infraction is felt most deeply, and *why* such an impression is made by the "unsporting". Let's take a third example, from an earlier round of the competition in which Suarez, in his own gloating words, made the "save of the tournament".

Having stuttered through the group stages, England were drawn to face Germany's exciting young team in Bloemfontein. Having watched Fabio Capello's side play out lethargic draws against the United States and Algeria, before scraping a 1–0 win over a poor Slovenia, most in England were aware that they would struggle against the likes of Özil, Klose, Schweinsteiger and Muller. Indeed, Germany had built up a 2–0 lead with only a third of the game gone when England fought their way back into the match. Matthew Upson scored in the 37th minute, and two minutes later Frank Lampard cracked a shot from the edge of the area which hit the underside of the bar, crossed the line, but rebounded into play. The referee and his assistant failed to register the goal, England stayed behind and Germany proceeded to double their tally, eventually winning 4–1. Lampard's "ghost goal" became the counterpart in Anglo-German footballing mythology to Geoff Hurst's eternally dubious strike in the final at Wembley in 1966, when the ball appeared to hit the goal-line but was perceived by the Azerbaijani linesman to have crossed it. On that occasion, England beat Germany to the World Cup; in South Africa, the decision was regarded by many English supporters as having cost their team the game, or at least a fair go at winning it, and the path was set conclusively for the introduction of goal-line technology both in the Premier League and the World Cup.

As their name suggests, ghost goals are an uncanny experience: they're neither *of* nor *outside* the game. They're not counted as an event within play, but the "outside" of play registers them as physical occurrences within the play-world. Metaphors for the sensation they produce are most usefully found in art, such as when a play or film breaks the fourth wall, perhaps, or – even more pertinently – when Kafka's fiction produces what Theodor Adorno calls a "shudder" on the part of the reader by reintroducing the world. In Kafka's *The Castle*, a novel which seems to be set in a purely allegorical space, a village which is simultaneously anywhere and nowhere, a vertiginous effect is produced when real-world locations are mentioned such as Spain and southern France. This does not affect us, I think, because we are suddenly forced to confront the idea that the sickeningly bizarre events Kafka talks about are happening in our world – we generally know the difference between the world of life and representations of that world – but because the text has, up to that point, established a code which implies that it operates somewhere whose existential being is as stable and autonomous as we believe our own to be. When real European locations are mentioned, the rule of spacelessness which gave us a handle on how to read the text is not only compromised, but shown to be completely impotent.

This sudden perception of the impotence of a governing code or an interpretative key is surely how we feel when we realise that football's rules can by no means account for every possibility that is generated within a game. Bearing this in mind, perhaps a claim can be made that a significant degree of football's force as a public experience comes about when it transgresses itself, when it shows itself to be beyond prediction or technocratic regulation. Monitors can be installed on goal-lines and games can be paused to get second opinions from officials in the stands with high-res monitors, but something will always occur which belongs not to the match itself, but to the metagame. In tabletop and roleplaying games, "metagaming" refers to the deployment by human players of information that is not available to the characters within the game-world. A player, for example, might not send his character into a dungeon where he knows there is a dragon because he might recently have fallen out in real life with the gamesmaster, who he suspects might now be more likely to tilt any battle in the dragon's favour. Play proceeds, then, not according to a game's intrinsic logic, but on the other side of its skin. Consider Suarez at the 2010 World Cup once more: his decision to handle the ball on the line – and this is not an infrequent occurrence; I've seen it take place in real life, both as a spectator and as a player – exploited the compositional finitude of the rules and was based on his understanding that his side would not be removed from the tournament for an in-game infringement. While the world of the match asks its participants to act in good faith by forgetting the broader competitive and social context, and thus maintain the Corinthian ideal of complete commitment to the singular encounter, the structure of formal competition introduces variables which come to bear on the internal poetics of the game.

Indeed, the registers and temporalities of, respectively, the match and the competition contradict one another. In Chapter One, I made this point to think about how competitive football's duration replicates the ceaseless creative destruction of capitalism which, in the views of theorists of modernity such as Baudelaire and Benjamin, resulted in the repetitive vaporisation of the moment producing a constant sense of loss. Victory in the match is no longer Corinthian, pointing towards abstract concepts such as glory, but takes its part in a campaign structure which can bring to bear any number of real-world exigencies on the individual match. It doesn't take us long to think of examples of this. Until Germany's victory in 2014, for example, no European team had won a World Cup staged in the Americas, and only the exceptional Brazilian team of 1958 had won a European-held World Cup for South America. If the sample size was small, with only two or three competitions in either region, we might be able to overlook this, but the World Cup is now such a long-running affair that numerous countries (France, Mexico, Brazil, Germany and Italy) have been able to host it twice. This, then, is the most glaring proof that the game, in the sense of what takes place within the markings of the pitch and in ninety, or one hundred and twenty, minutes, is thoroughly ill-equipped to keep out contingency. The Laws of the Game are written almost as if matches take place in vacuums, each constituting a perfect, existentially unique world, but any given game will tend to disprove this. Ironically, of course, it was this very attempt to produce a Platonic standard for football that led to the fact of competition, which vastly multiplied contingency!

The closest football has come to achieving the hermetic game implied by the rules is not in the no-stakes pre-season friendly, but in the early computer simulations in which poor game physics and bad AI, plus a non-competitive "Single Match" mode, reduced football to a one-off encounter without individual player psychology, specific local or atmospheric interferences, or a crowd composed of anything more than thousands of replicated bobbing white circles. More sophisticated modern computer simulations have encountered something of a paradox in their attempts to achieve a higher degree of realism, in that to reach such a plane of verisimilitude vast amounts of contingency would have to be introduced which would then undermine, possibly to the extent of cancelling out, the human player's ability to win matches using their coordination and dexterity. Indeed, if one plays the latest edition of FIFA or Pro Evolution Soccer, by far the market leaders in the competition to accurately simulate football, they have masked this problem by introducing simulacra of contingency by realistically rendering the faces of individual players, thus implying psychology, and the architecture of real-world stadia, thus suggesting a social reality imposing itself on the matches played.

Football-management simulations, the most famous version of which is *Football Manager*, formerly known as *Championship Manager*, have a different set of mechanics to deal with the question of the social, political and human parts of football. Because the player does not have to control the team in the virtual "real time" of matches, making the strikers shoot and the defenders tackle, there is no risk of their well-honed hand-to-eye skills being undermined. Instead, the up-to-date editions of management games, which are in effect enormous, playable spreadsheets, build in the effect of contingency as one of the significant obstacles human players must overcome. Ever since the beginning of the *Championship Manager* series in the early 1990s, there was a (slim) possibility that a star player would be injured for a long time by circumstances completely beyond your control, but nowadays one must cope with the media, who can spread rumours to unsettle a squad, temperamental individuals and, most tellingly, the off-field economics of the club you control.

Once again, though, this is fake contingency. The mechanics of *Football Manager* do not provide for macro-economic events such as the ITV Digital crisis of 2002, which had a terrible effect on the finances of many lower-league English clubs. While in real life, the post-2008 situation has exerted huge pressure on football, a serious football-management game simply would not write the possibility of such an event into its code, understanding, rightly, that this level of unpredictability would be perceived as unfair by the player. "Realism" in any football game is, then, only the attempt to reduce football to a series of relatively predictable mechanics resistant to the real world and then represent these in a way which appears close to a (stabilised version of) life. How would a player feel if, having reached a virtual World Cup final in Colombia or Argentina using England or Italy, they opened the pre-match team-selection screen to find all of their players depleted of energy because, in the non-controllable, megatextual game "reality", local fans had gathered outside the team hotel to make noise all night? Remember the occasion when Tottenham, needing to win on the final day of the season against West Ham to secure a place in the Champions League, were struck down by norovirus and therefore forced to field a number of second-stringers and walking sick? Again, that would seem, in a game, like a rather draconian wielding of realistic consequentiality.

Simulations of the game, as with most commercially available simulations of anything, must somehow produce the illusion of contingency without allowing any actual contingency; that is, they must deploy what Roland Barthes called the "reality effect". The "reality effect" in mimetic art works on the principle that what gives real life its character is the sheer amount of material we encounter which is not "notable", which has no significant meaning for us as we go about our lives. To capture this, fiction, theatre and film must give us details which exceed the narrative's structure of meaning and which are not recuperated by some final symbolic "message". The genuinely inconsequential detail in a piece of narrative art is made to stand for contingency in general, that which disrupts stable meaning-making. In simulation, the same thing holds: because a game falls to pieces if it admits true contingency, it seeks strategies to denote it through synecdoche, through little fragments of the complexity and dynamism of reality.

*Real* football, by contrast, is, at its most fascinating, a structure so fragile that it seems at times to be acting as a blank screen onto which the whole drama of exigency can be projected. At the beginning of Chapter One, I used the story of the dogs on the pitch at Galatasaray to illustrate how football might be used in the classroom or lecture theatre as an apparently frivolous, apparently low-cultural analogical tool for unpacking high theory's complexity. Returning to this vignette, it's possible to say that it counts for far more than just that, because it can be an emblem of how the true essence of the game lies in its susceptibility to what is nominally outside it. By this, I'm not referring to the efforts we make to load football with abstract significance, to make it "mean something" within the auspices of a wider patriotic or otherwise political project. These attempts sometimes succeed and sometimes fail, and there is little doubt that football can be mobilised significantly to both reactionary and progressive ends. Argentina's victory in the 1978 Men's World Cup shored up the legitimacy of the Junta; the recent success of England's women's team in the 2015 Women's World Cup will hopefully act as a counter to the UK's ongoing culture of persistent, low-level sexism. Regardless, these are *uses* of football which pertain to its outside, rather than a demonstration of how we perceive football most directly when the outside emerges erratically, even capriciously, within it.

More dogs. In 1987, on the last day of the season in the old Fourth Division of the English Football League, Torquay United needed to draw to avoid relegation. They were losing 2–1 to Crewe when, deep in the second half, a police dog which was being used to attend to trouble in the ground bit one of their defenders. In the five minutes of injury time which resulted, Torquay equalised, meaning that Lincoln were relegated in their place. Subsequently, and ever since in fact, the story of that day has been "the dog that saved a football club from relegation", which is not particularly true, given that any league match is played out over the same amount of time if the referee's watch is working. Torquay did not get "extra time" as such, it's just the five minutes of playing time occurred slightly later in terms of clock-time than it was scheduled to. Nevertheless, it has been considered fitting to narrate the tale *post facto* in a way that emphasises, rather than honestly downplays, the role of contingency, unruliness, disorder, transgression and coincidence. A game like this, or the one in which Lampard "scored" his "ghost goal", or when Suarez handballed on the line, is as likely to provide "the one moment – the one match" as one in which an instance of entirely legitimate virtuosity occurs, and perhaps it is even more so.

However, contingency, by definition, is resistant to the logic of privatisation and the commodity. Running out of product, capital tries: think of how the tech industry attempts to sell its latest tablets, phones and cameras on the basis that they have a superior capacity for recording the most whimsical of events. But this is not the same thing as being dependably able to handcraft the Kafkian shudder, to rationalise the irrational. In lieu of doing this, football can only be fully privatised if it is sealed hermetically against contingency and made subject to the full spectrum of empirical analysis. A turn in this direction has occurred over the last decade, and it is one which has appeared, to many supporters, as largely benign.

We know all about the success of Sabermetrics, the statistics-based approach to recruitment in baseball pioneered by Billy Beane, thanks to the book and film *Moneyball*. Beane has been hailed by some as a heroic democratiser of sports because his highly empirical, almost aggressively data-centred methodology allows smaller clubs to acquire players who might have slipped the attention of coaches and scouts whose heads are turned by the spectacular. By prioritising effectiveness and consistency over the melodramatic brilliance of the moment, Sabermetrics allows non-elite teams to extract maximum value from their financial resources and challenge at the top. While statistics first came to prominence in American sports – which tend to lend themselves to empirical analysis to a greater extent than football, whose long passages of play conceal many nuances which are hard to quantify – they have gradually become ensconced in the game's strategic repertoire.

The groundwork for the quantification of football began in a way which felt like innocuous fun at the time. In the early 1990s, newspapers began running Fantasy Football tournaments, in which readers paid to participate in a competition where they used a budget to assemble an imaginary, usually humorously named, team from a list of existing players. The players' values were based largely on empirical data, namely the number of goals they had scored and "assists" they had produced in the previous season, and the number of "clean sheets" they had kept if they played in defensive positions. What was, and still is, interesting about newspaper Fantasy Football is that the values do not correspond exactly to stats, because big-name players seem to cost more than less well-known peers whose statistics are better. Nevertheless, despite this odd game mechanic, the pastime introduced the football-supporting public to the kind of statistical presentation American sports fans have been used to for decades, and, in particular, suggested that creativity was a quality which could be known numerically rather than intuitively thanks to the all-important "assists" column.

Once the public had become accustomed to this mathematical perspective on something they had hitherto registered according to all kinds of unmethodical interpretation, it was the turn of actual managers. Mid-ranking teams became interested in marginal gains, hiring performance analysts who could identify ways in which a squad lacking, at least in comparison to the top clubs, in talent could make the best use of their assets. Latterly, Beane's dogma has been brought into these clubs to allow them to navigate the transfer market successfully, and one team designed entirely according to Sabermetric principles, FC Midtjylland, have recently won Denmark's top division. With the increasing interest of managers, coaches and directors of football in an ever-diversifying range of metrics that can be used in this neo-Victorian attempt to reduce all aspects of play to a taxonomy, there has been a concomitant growth in the football statistics industry epitomised by companies like Squawka. Such organisations have two main customer bases, football professionals who require sophisticated data for the reasons specified above, and high-stakes gamblers who are looking for nuanced prediction models.

Much of the debate around Squawka and their competitors in the stats market is how they disenchant the game by dismissing so much of what fans take pleasure in as inutile. Few people who watch football regularly don't know the pleasure of having a personal favourite player, someone out on the pitch for whom a completely irrational admiration is developed. While statistics might prove that our hunch about a player is justified at the level of numerical contribution, they can easily do the opposite, robbing us of our illusions by demonstrating that someone we thought was contributing because of their aesthetically enjoyable style of play is a mere luxury as far as the team is concerned. Nevertheless, their potential to disabuse is a secondary form of harm when considered alongside their representation of football as something which can be known by its internal workings alone. Listening to the most evangelical advocates of Sabermetrics talk about football, it's hard to believe that they're discussing the same sport. Their particular mode of scrutiny could lead you to think that nobody had ever sung a song, waved a banner, set off a flare, laughed or cried in a stadium; in fact, it could convince you that football took place in a true vacuum, that it occurred in a genuinely private space, cut off from all sociality.

It should be obvious why this is worrying. Corporate concerns within football are acted upon in a relationship of constant and unwavering hostility to fans, particularly now that the income generated by spectators paying at the gate is, for the biggest clubs at least, dwarfed by that brought in by television rights, branded merchandise and increasingly surreal link-ups with business. Manchester United, to name a persistent offender, have an "official tire partner for Asia", a relationship which would have been inconceivable fifteen years ago but is now merely representative of how elite clubs make money. By diminishing the social aspects of the game, the Beane-counters play directly into the hands of corporate interests which tend to regard matchgoing fans at best as a source of pin money and at worst, and more usually, as a nuisance to be subdued.

Another confirmation of the sense that a technocracy is emerging, this time occurring amongst fans and journalists, is the heightened interest in tactical nuances. This is perhaps a more uneasy topic, as the writers who have created something of a scene around playing systems, a modish *tactocracy*, are true fans of the game who, presumably, have no wish for it to be further commodified. Indeed, a number of those who have written detailed accounts of tactical development, not least the *Guardian* writer Jonathan Wilson, have also produced exacting studies of football in its historical and social contexts. Wilson developed his reputation with two books. The first, *Behind the Curtain*, was a wide-ranging investigation of the effects of the end of communism on football in Eastern and Central Europe, while the second, *Inverting the Pyramid*, looked at trends in tactics from the beginning of the game to the modern day. He is clearly a commentator who sees football in the round, taking an interest both in its various on-pitch permutations and in the way that social, political and economic change is brought to bear on the actual playing of the game. Nevertheless, his imitators have developed a style of writing which increasingly diminishes the effect of the social and, once again, seeks to re-envision football as something which can be fully known, and therefore anticipated, so long as an adequate model is used. Consequently, their writing adds subtle assistance to corporate efforts to carry out one final, giant commodification. Those who take an interest in tactics are, unlike other spectators, actually advantaged by not being at the game and instead watching on television, because television allows for camera angles which are holistic and can depict the whole shape of a team. Replay functions can also emphasise tactical subtleties that would go unnoticed by fans watching in real time within the stadium. Tactocracy, then, covertly suggests that *actually going to the game* is not the ideal form of encounter with football, as to do so limits the possibilities of solipsistic, top-down, "objective" analysis of the match because it involves distracting social encounters.

What we have seen emerge over the last decade, in both the importation of Sabremetrics from American sport and the growth of tactical literacy from a simple "interest" into something almost sinister and cultish, represents a form of footballing puritanism, an attempt to speak of the sport as though it were always played in laboratory conditions, to Corinthian standards. It's a puritanism, however, which has the effect of transforming its object of worship into a product, of removing contingency, and with it the trace of the local and the particular. By pushing football back towards its universal form, the game's antagonistic aspect is removed. One might deplore Suarez or Maradona for their acts of rebellion, and bemoan the referee and assistant referees that cost Frank Lampard his goal in Bloemfontein, but there is a way in which all of these individuals were, through error or malice, keeping football true to its historical role as a globally ubiquitous frame of particularity. Technocracy, by which politics is turned into a matter of allegedly "objective" expertise, works throughout Europe in the 21st century as an apparatus by which a neoliberal consensus is maintained: we're asked to trust a cadre of economic specialists, all of whom turn out to come in favour of more austerity, more privatisation. Why shouldn't the same process be at work in sport? Brian Clough's dismissal of the voluminous "crap talked about tactics by people who barely know how to win at dominoes" was funny, but surely did not anticipate the way in which the same people would ultimately, if inadvertently, work in the favour of granting big business even more agency within football.

# GAIS 0 – Hammarby 0

## 26 OCTOBER 2014

It was a lunchtime start at the Gamla Ullevi and cold, fine rain was blowing across Skånegatan, the arterial road skirting Gothenburg city centre. In the small hours of the previous night I'd arrived in town without my bags, thanks to a computer error at Heathrow; consequently, I'd spent my first morning – the Sunday morning after the autumn clock change – in a new country shopping for new clothes for meetings with new colleagues. Nevertheless, I was still determined to watch some football. Going up and down the main boulevard in a state of mounting sartorial anxiety, I'd seen hundreds of people in the black and green colours of the host club, GAIS, a fair few visitors from Stockholm's Hammarby, and more riot police than I'd ever encountered. A police helicopter hung against the Kattegat gloom.

All this made it strange when I arrived at the stadium three quarters of an hour before kick-off to find the gates barred and padlocked. Peering through at pitch level into the vast, Fifties brutalist arena, I saw no evidence of any activity – no open kiosks, no stewards, no warm-up. If I'd been in Britain, I'd have come to the conclusion that the rain had overcome the match, or that I'd made some outrageous calendarial misunderstanding, but, when I'm acclimatising to an unfamiliar country, I generally offer a deadpan acceptance of what I see and try to work with it. With a trust-to-the-winds stoicism, I dawdled round the stadium perimeter for a while, only gradually establishing what had happened. I was at the wrong ground. This was the Nya Ullevi, used for big concerts, the games the Swedish national team stage in Gothenburg, and Champions League matches if the city's biggest side,

103

IFK, qualify. The *Gamla* Ullevi – more modern and compact – was a few hundred yards down the road. Now pretty soaked, I doubled my pace, a little pleased at having a ready-made lede for anything I wrote about the game, and bought a ticket for 150 *kronor*, about thirteen pounds.

Not that this purchased access with any convenience. All the home supporters were being filtered, painstakingly, through one entryway in the direction of a double checkpoint of security and police. There had been trouble between these sides before, and Hammarby had brought a huge contingent of their support across to the Swedish west coast. It was the penultimate game of the season (like Norway, Iceland and Ireland's, Sweden's is a summer league) and the visitors needed to win to guarantee promotion from the second-echelon Superettan, a level that, at least on the basis of their following, they were far too big for. GAIS are also, by Swedish standards, quite well-backed, and tend to see themselves as the authentic representatives of Gothenburg's working class, with some of their fans embracing the increasingly familiar St-Pauli-of-X football-punk aesthetic.

Reading up for information about the game beforehand, I couldn't quite figure out how these teams, who seemed to have obvious sociocultural affinities, had managed to confect a rivalry. Sceptically, I wondered if this was part of a Scandinavian tradition of importing youth culture from the UK. Gothenburg might resemble Newcastle or Glasgow in some important respects, but it is clearly more affluent, or is better at levelling the affluence it has, and the idea of football violence as some post-punk expression of disenfranchisement seemed a little ludicrous here. Perhaps because the regions have proved slightly more resistant than Britain to the sociopocalypse of neoliberalism, I've always, naively, thought of hooliganism in Scandinavia and German-speaking central Europe as absurd and petulant. Without a Thatcher or a Berlusconi, how could it be meaningful?

Nevertheless, the police and stewards were taking it seriously. In Adidas, Levis and a dark-blue cagoule, the only clothes I had after losing my bag but the ones I'd have probably worn for the game regardless, I was inviting a search, but I'd not been scanned for explosive residue at football before. After getting through the cordon, I headed into the concourse, only to shatter the image of cosmopolitan confidence I was trying to project by realising I had no idea where I was meant to be sitting and asking an old guy in a baseball cap, despite not even having enough Swedish to say "excuse me". He responded in perfect English: I could go anywhere in the stadium, except on the mysteriously closed terrace behind one goal or with the Hammarby fans (who were taking up one and a half of the stands). I chose a seat in the corner next to the unused section, behind a group of Londoners who, it turned out, had a horse in the race – their friend was playing on the wing for GAIS.

The substitutes finished the last of their lukewarm pre-match routines and left the pitch. While Hammarby could escape the Superettan for their more traditional berth in the Allsvenskan, GAIS were, as the saying goes, *looking over their shoulders* and desperately in need of something from the game. Above the tunnel to the changing rooms, in the centre of the long tribune, their ultras had gathered, trying to make some noise to drown out the welling racket from the Stockholm side's eye-catching *tifosi* behind the far goal. Again, I wondered why they weren't on the empty terrace. As the sides came onto the pitch, it became clear that, in fact, some kind of protest was being staged, and that it was related somehow to the vacant area below me. A superabundance of green flares were lit – the "beauty" of ultra culture is that the pyrotechnics always find their way in regardless – drenching the interior of the stand in smoke, with a couple being thrown onto the pitch, creating so much fog that the referee took the players off again. Older guys walked up and down the seating, exhorting everyone to stand and sing.

It's hard not to come to the conclusion that the outstanding motive of the ultra *capo* in European football is self-importance. The romantic line of football tourism is that ultra culture is something to be considered separately from both British football hooliganism (in spite of the obvious fetish for a 1980s "Golden Age" amongst the ultras, manifested not least in the English names of many groups) and "scarfer" supporting. I can just about see how this difference holds in, say, Egypt or Turkey, where massive ultra groups from clubs like Al-Ahly and Besiktas have played significant roles in anti-government movements: on a political level, they may well be more organised than their counterparts in the UK. In northern Europe, however, the bald men sitting on fences, backs to the game, leading chants through megaphones have a bumptiousness which, were they English, we'd be quick to compare to *Dad's Army*'s Captain Mainwaring. The "rebellion", however physically tough it might be and however much it can drink, is fastidious: we hear plenty of talk of the "choreography" of *tifo* displays, but there's also a sense in which the behaviour of individuals is choreographed by an extremely predictable set of instructions.

At the other end of the stadium, much the same was happening with the Hammarby fans, even if their *capos* were making a far better fist of getting their "troops" to sing in unison. As a spectacle, a large body of ultras acting in precise synchrony is an undeniably striking thing. It represents a visual and auditory force harnessed to a show of fierce fidelity which, for the idealist, might look more than a little like the spirit of the worker in its distilled and most politically febrile form. Yet this febrility, for the most part, only *looks* political in any meaningful sense and, frequently, when it does become politicised, attaches itself to reactionary causes, from anti-immigrant activity to, in the worst cases, interethnic conflict of the type witnessed in the Balkans in the 1990s and in Ukraine in the present day. Discussions about the "usefulness" of the ultra movement on the left – and there are, of course, a number of clubs across the continent where left-leaning ultras prevail – need to begin by recognising its massive instability. Moreover, to what extent does the cart pull the horse here? Does the political cause simply become a point of order? Is it used to authenticate, validate or justify the "real" aim of following the club?

Watching expensively dressed grandfathers in one of the wealthiest countries in the world incite a crowd to offer to – at least so it appeared – lay their lives on the line of a sporting cause, I was once again assailed by a biting sense of ridiculousness. I'd been to hundreds of games in the last few seasons and offered vociferous, sometimes personally draining support to two clubs, but as an outsider the point was escaping me. On the pitch, GAIS and Hammarby were playing out one of the worst games I'd seen for years, a contest between two sides keen not to lose and set up to absorb pressure. Neither team had a forward quick enough to spring the offside trap; the only class on the pitch came from Hammarby's former Swedish international midfielder, and my almost-namesake, Kennedy Bakircioglü. The balding Bakircioglü is perhaps most famous in the Anglosphere for his reliable excellence in mid-period installations of the PC football-management simulator *Championship Manager*, and anybody – like me – who played the game in the early 2000s has probably fielded him at some point. It was strange to see him in real life, where he played, and looked, like some cruise-ship tribute to Zinedine Zidane, trying to nudge the incompetence around him into some sort of shape while hunting for opportunities to hit cross-field passes or lash a shot at the underworked GAIS goalkeeper.

The drizzle worsened with the game. I'd expected, and even hoped, for this weather: in my mind, the romance of Gothenburg was to be of drab outsides and austerely snug bourgeois interiors, the strangely morbid dream of Scandinavia that British people have produced by conflating Ibsen with *Wallander* and *The*

*Killing*. The Gamla Ullevi didn't really fit into this schema, but it was accommodated comfortably by another. Aside from the two sections of safe standing behind the goals, it was the picture of the contemporary medium-sized football ground, a symmetrical and rationalised space for watching the match and going home punctually. The ultras only intensified this sense: they were absolutely integral to what in Britain is increasingly called the "matchday experience". While a game in the Swedish second division hardly represents the pinnacle of football's commodification, this is more because of the sheer scale of commodification that has affected the top level of European football than because of any inherent imperviousness on the part of secondary leagues and nations. The Superettan was no exception to the general rule of the market.

Leaving the game, which finished as scorelessly as it had promised to in the terrible first half, I walked up to the square in front of the central station. The police were still present in substantial numbers, but any threat of trouble had passed, and the Hammarby supporters were being sent back across the country by train and bus in an orderly manner. For the British fan who mostly consumes football via the television, there is perhaps something exotic, if obscurantist, about attending a fixture like this, but it seemed very close to home, an experience as formulaic as the one I'd had at St James' ten months previously. Perhaps it was exhaustion at having attended so many games over the preceding couple of years paired with excitement at a relatively new job and a shifting set of priorities, but the footballing optimism of the previous summer was beginning to wear off.

Then again, isn't that what I've been trying to argue here? That the true political potential of football lies not in its capacity for fulfilment and plenitude, but in the fact that it frustrates, withholding what we think we want at the precise moment we feel we need it the most? Isn't football the location of a radicalised disappointment which can produce a solidarity and empathy far in excess of the so-called "cause" of sporting victory? Ultimately, the solution towards which football points is that football itself cannot be the solution. It can offer us fragmented visions of utopia, but the key to resisting the way in which it is mobilised ideologically is to remember that these visions are microcosms which refuse to become general unless everything else is rectified. Power tells us that football is a cause for blind loyalty to which everything else should be subordinated, hence the advertorial focus on *passion* and *commitment* and *the shirt*. It suggests that football is where – and the only place where – we will find earthly fulfilment, and this, perhaps, is the tragedy of the ultras: that they have subscribed to this. Football can bring joy, of course, but the idea that this joy is *only* to do with football, that the game possesses an authenticity which exceeds anything politics and history have to offer, gets it the wrong way round. Football's joy is historical joy, political joy, a vantage point on a better life rather than something in and for itself.

# CHAPTER FOUR

# Bad Wools and Plastics: Authenticity and Football's "Distribution of the Sensible"

*We* are the true supporters.
– LEEDS FAN CHANT, 1970s

It's very easy, when you feel you've really paid your dues as a football fan, to laugh along at parodies of latecomers to the game. One of the funniest of these comes in a song from the album *Ninety Bisodol (Crimond)* by old-hand Birkenhead post-punks Half Man Half Biscuit, an act who have made this trope a running gag. It's called 'Rock and Roll is Full of Bad Wools', and its first verse tells the story of the downfall of an aspirantly geezerish indie musician making his first appearance on a banal, football-themed Saturday morning panel show. Asked who he supports, the singer responds predictably: he's a fan of "England" (obviously), "Chelsea" (who win), "Accy Stanley" (the East Lancashire club who have had a comic reputation for badness since featuring on a 1980s milk advertisement) and "Barca" (who "all the band love watching", because who doesn't). But catastrophe strikes. The presenter notes that "he comes from Leigh-on-Sea" and asks him if he ever "gets to Roots Hall" to watch Southend United, his unglamorous local team. To him, this "means fuck all"; humiliated, his nascent career is in tatters.

Half Man Half Biscuit are full-time supporters of the typically struggling Merseyside club Tranmere Rovers, and part of their mythology and mystique is that they supposedly turned down their one chance to be on *Top of the Pops* because the recording of the programme clashed with a Rovers fixture. In their songs, it's clear that the part-timers, the glory supporters and "types who never used to go to the match until the family thing got big in the late Eighties" fit into their rogues' gallery of bourgeois dilettantism: other frequent targets include faddish world-music listeners, vegan parents and student nihilists. The football bandwagon is just one more site in which the middle classes can play out their drama of agitated appropriation.

Looking back to the early 1990s, it's clear that, not least in the case of Nick Hornby, a gap began to open between middle-class football fans and those who, at least implicitly, are framed by HMHB and other sites of Prole Art Threat satire such as *Viz* magazine as "proper" supporters. The publication of *Fever Pitch*, the water-cooler success of Italia '90, the return of British clubs into post-*Glasnost* Europe, and the advent of the new, user-friendly Premier League created an environment in which so-called "plastics" – floating supporters who could commit to football purely as leisure or entertainment – could thrive. Undoubtedly, it was football's ability to attract this constituency which "necessitated" the increasing commodification and gentrification of the game and its stadia, a process which has moved very quickly from a situation in which the put-down "glory supporters" denoted Surrey-based Manchester United fans to one where it implicates the legions of deep-pocketed tourists visiting Liverpool and Chelsea from China and Thailand every weekend.

As such, it seems predictable enough that longstanding supporters, particularly in the Premier League, feel some resentment towards middle-class gentrifiers and those who have followed in their wake. Authenticity has become the watchword in a battle for football's elusive "soul", with old-timers frequently using social media to emphasise, in ways which vary in subtlety, the depth and *truth* of their affinity for the club in question.

Look – and I offer this advice with the caveat that it is over-whelmingly a depressing experience – at the online discussion forums devoted to Liverpool, a club at which the current authen-ticity wars are only an intensification of a conflict which dates to their national and European dominance in the 1970s and 1980s. The inexorable conflict between true Scousers from Liverpool and "wools", a term once used at Anfield to mock fans from west Lancashire, Cheshire and North Wales, has mutated into a bizarre competition in which Cornish and Norwegian fans try to prove their merit by using ever-increasingly arcane forms of Merseyside dialect to score points off the supposed fakes. Noth-ing is more toxic amongst modern football fans than the suspi-cion that you're not "real".

A lack of "reality" has been a common complaint amongst fans both in Britain and further afield in the last twenty years. The Italian slogan *No al calcio moderno* has morphed of late into the English "Against Modern Football", a battle-cry which has been taken up not only by Premier League fans weary of exces-sive ticket prices and commercialisation but by supporters of lower-league and non-league football wary of the baleful trick-le-down effects of changes at the top. One way in which the atti-tudes implied by "modern football" have been resisted has been in the drawing of battle lines designed to separate "true" and "plastic" modes of supporting. Inspired by European ultra cul-ture, or at least by an interpretation of European ultra culture based to a degree on hearsay and mythology, fans have tried to create dedicated "singing sections" in all-seated stadia. The par-aphernalia of ultra fandom – declamatory banners, smoke canis-ters and flares – have become regular sights in British grounds, and younger supporters have embraced the fashion staples of the '80s casuals: Adidas, Lyle & Scott, Harrington jackets and cagoules have all returned emphatically. Un-modern football, then, might in some quarters be sketched out as an uneasy syncretisation of two forms of supporter practice, namely '80s hooliganism and contemporary European *ultraismo*.

This is where #AMF, to give it its rightful hashtag, becomes interesting. On one hand, it seems to be a genuine expression of annoyance at the sense that the game has been stolen by capitalism or, to be more accurate, has been stolen from localised industrial capitalism by global hypercapitalism. In many ways correctly, it sees the alleged comforts of modern grounds, the leather-coated seats and the expensive hot-dog stands, as economic provocations designed to drive working-class "traditional" fans from clubs by putting the majority of the "matchday experience" beyond their financial wherewithal. It resists the way in which the game is expected to dance to capital's whims, and its primary spokespeople (in the UK, journalists like David Conn, David Goldblatt and Martin Cloake) have succeeded at least in getting a hearing, however cursory, from some of those at the top table of football. But #AMF is two-sided, and the reverse of the social-democratic hopefulness emblematised by those named above, optimists driven by a recollection of the best aspects of football before neoliberalism, is a reactionary tendency resistant to attempts to cleanse the game of discriminatory attitudes. This will ultimately bear consideration in relation to the broader problems confronted by social-democratic politics, but should first be illustrated with some examples of reactionary traditionalism.

In August 2014, James McMahon, the editor of UK heavy-metal magazine *Kerrang!*, published an article in the left-leaning *New Statesman* in which he renounced his support of Leyton Orient, a club then playing in League One, the third division of English football. The incident which provoked this was the response to a series of Tweets he made complaining about fellow Orient supporters singing a song about the glories of East London, a place supposedly abundant in "tits, fannies and football". As he points out in the article, it's certainly not the most atavistic number in the repertoire of English football fans, but it possesses the capacity to make female supporters feel deeply uncomfortable and unwelcome in its between-the-lines assumption of a male audience. Consequently, it claims the stadium as an exclusively male space. McMahon was, he writes, subsequently subjected to gratuitous online abuse (the terrace favourite "nonce", "fat cunt" and much, much more in a similar vein) and instructed that the song he was offended by was simply "banter". Pointedly, he was told that he was "ruining football".

This is representative of the beliefs of the right flank of the #AMF constellation. Here, the commercialisation of the game is conflated with efforts to make it accessible to the point at which anti-racism, anti-homophobia and (perhaps particularly) anti-misogyny are represented as the root of a decline in atmosphere. The blame is shunted leftwards while the progressive potential of the anti-commercial sentiments is absorbed by a right-wing politics reminiscent of blogger Splintering Bone Ashes' original description of "negative solidarity". Negative solidarity, as initially conceived, is what happens when working-class solidarity is contingent not on a shared experience of exploitation at the hands of a capitalist property-owning class, but on an affective experience of resentment at the perceived "advantages" of (for example) benefits claimants or asylum seekers. One of the greatest obstacles posed by a politics of negative solidarity is that it advances a position that is objectively reactionary but makes this unanswerable via a logic of authenticity: if "real" people resent benefit claimants or asylum seekers, then how can you say that a politics which discriminates against them is undesirable? Likewise, if "real" football fans say anti-racism or anti-sexism – rather than a corrupt structure of governance, commercially fixated management or plutocratic owners – are to blame, who are we to challenge them?

In a similar period, a comparable and related issue afflicted the non-league game, which, viewed from certain angles, has thrived in recent years with an influx of supporters disillusioned by its commercialised professional counterpart. At a number of clubs, resistance both to football's neoliberalisation and to various modes of bigotry has become a rallying point: it might be argued that FC United of Manchester were founded on such lines, while, in inner London, two clubs in particular have received attention for what is perceived as a left-wing terrace culture. The first of these, whose following is bigger but less coherently political, is the Southwark side Dulwich Hamlet, who have already been covered at some length in this book. The second is Clapton F.C., who compete in the Essex Senior League (the *ninth* level of English football!) in Forest Gate in the East End borough of Newham. Since the 2012–2013 season, Clapton's two-figure regular support has been bolstered considerably by a group identifying as the "Clapton Ultras", an alliance of up to several hundred mostly young fans who take advantage of cheap tickets and lax stadium regulations both to create a facsimile of European antifascist *ultraismo* of the sort seen at St Pauli, Rayo Vallecano, and Livorno, and to hollow out within organised, competitive men's football a non-discriminatory safe space in which all genders, ethnicities and sexual orientations are made welcome.

In the cases of both Dulwich and Clapton, the development of a different kind of supporter culture to the one we're used to in the English game can be explained by socioeconomic factors which hinge on the twin poles of the UK's over-centralised economy and the demographics of gentrification. London has always been the gravitational point of employment in Britain, but never more so than in the era of austerity and excessive tuition fees, when many young people gamble on surviving the capital's vastly inflated rental market to earn the elevated wages which might give them at least a fighting chance of entering their forties out of debt. The streets might not be paved with gold, but the jobs market works disproportionately in favour of London, and it is also more or less the sole point of ingress for people wanting to work in the media or the creative industries. As such, the few areas of inner London (Hackney, Southwark and Lewisham) which had not already been fully gentrified have, in the last decade, become home to a twenty- and thirty-something class of low-paid professionals, arts post-graduates, fixed-term "creatives" and precarious workers.

In the popular imagination, this social phenomenon has become cluttered with narratives about the urban hipster, and there is certainly some crossover, as there is with the group of provenance-fixated, beard-wearing *anti-hipsters* frequently con-fused with hipsters. Consequently, the young inhabitants of Peck-ham, Camberwell and Dalston are construed in terms of a set of erroneously conflated stereotypes: they're postmodern ironists drinking microbrewed beer, Grizzly Adams wannabes listening to white-label techno. These characterisations are produced to an industrial scale and are perpetuated by a class of more secure, well-paid and in some cases slightly older professionals, those who genuinely are advantaged by gentrification and who need to find an easy, satirically fecund alibi for their economic privilege. Read, for example, the Men's pages of the *Daily Telegraph* or the Culture pages of the *Evening Standard*, and you'll find a suspicious amount of grumbling about how "the local" only serves craft beer now, or how the "corner shop has been replaced by a burger joint". What looks like light-hearted social observation is, in reality, an attempt to explain gentrification with a straw-man, a straw-man whose predominant foible is a lack of (usually poorly defined) "authenticity".

One of the reasons why this image has so much purchase is that, in a world where many university graduates find the kinds of material comfort their parents were able to access an unattain-able and even unimaginable goal – Slavoj Žižek talks about the "proletarianisation" of the young middle classes across Europe – the search for the real offers some kind of compensation. That's to say that, amongst a group criticised widely for their lack of authenticity, there's an entirely explicable commitment to the "authenticity" offered (on one hand) by cultural obscurantism and (on the other) by the back-to-the-land aesthetics and ethics of the artisan food movement. That which seems, however illusorily, to resemble some form of outside to the hypercapitalism of a city like London exerts a powerful attraction, and one site which offers a ready-made experience of the DIY, communitarian, para-punk ideal is non-league football. At both Dulwich and Clapton, a significant number of the newcomers are (like me) fans who have supported, often fervently and actively, professional clubs only to be put off by the factors of the cost of getting to a geographically distant ground from London and, more existentially, the revulsion at the commercialisation of even relatively low levels of English professional football.

The convenient myth, however, is that the success of both clubs in attracting new and substantial fanbases is down predominantly to newcomers who "know nothing about" and even "don't care about" football. Fans of Dulwich and Clapton's opponents have varied in their responses to having their sleepy suburban grounds taken over by pyro-wielding ultras – in many cases, they've proclaimed it a breath of fresh air – but the more snide attitudes have tended to focus on "hipsters". The suspicion is that this form of supporting, which takes as its starting point a desire for *more* realness, is deeply inauthentic.

Free from any question of politics, this would be surmountable. The problem comes when the allegations of inauthenticity become focused specifically on the left-wing politics of both groups of fans, a radicalism which ranges from the surrealist and satirical (Dulwich's DIY t-shirts have an aesthetic influenced in equal parts by P-funk, cyberpunk and Marxist sloganeering) to the actively, militantly antifascist. Shortly after Dulwich played a friendly against Stonewall FC, the UK's highest-ranking gay football team, the *Sunday Times* columnist Rod Liddle published an article which, while celebratory of the revival of a dormant South London non-league power, was dismissive of the supporter politics on show at Champion Hill, the club's home on the borders of East Dulwich and Camberwell. "There is something slightly nauseating", he wrote, "about the way in which the fans of this club have become detached from its working class roots". The fact notwithstanding that the match had been organised at the instigation of a longstanding, gay, working-class supporter brought up on the estate facing Champion Hill, Liddle's dog whistle was fairly easy to interpret. Working-class – that is "authentic" – beliefs are not compatible with a politics opposed to discrimination.

Again, one might just regard these claims as a hack's prerogative. But Liddle has significant form on this front: his columns are invariably pitched between blokey pub-and-Millwall stories and attacks on a largely imagined class of mandarins enforcing a dogma of political correctness on the (straw) common man. Despite the fact that, as a lead columnist for several Murdoch papers, Liddle is likely compensated with a salary several times that of the average attendee at Champion Hill, his golf-club "realism" produces an effect of authorial reliability. If you want your politics to have the patina of a popular mandate, counterpose them to those of the so-called hipsters. Diverting briefly into the thought of the contemporary French writer Jacques Rancière, this can be taken as an example of how the field of the political is, rather than the simple, isolable parliamentary process neoliberalism marks it out as, nothing less than the entire "distribution of the sensible", the management of what can be said and who can say it. Liddle, of course, would tell me that I'm speaking the "faux-intellectual" idiom of "trendy sociology" here, no doubt, but this would simply prove my point, namely that one should be extremely suspicious of any attempt to disparage critique on the grounds of authenticity.

Vague flippancy aside, the claim that an anti-homophobia initiative represents a detachment of non-league football from its "working-class roots" is obviously an example of *sense* being *distributed*, of an attempt to set the limits of what might be thought and expected both of and by a particular social stratum. In an apparently harmless article, full of Liddle's characteristic "banter", a chain of equivalence is produced between "roots" – an authentic ground – and a reactionary worldview. This equivalence has dictated the strategic course and the tactical tone of British, and particularly English, politics in the last decade, and will be examined in more detail after a short aside to consider how such examples of the distribution of the sensible have turned physical in Clapton's case.

In 2014 a group emerged online calling itself the Pie and Mash Squad. Formerly, they had been linked to the English Defence League fellow travellers Casuals United, a pan-UK organisation which aimed to bring together the members of rival casual firms to oppose the supposed threat of Islamic fundamentalism in Britain. Like the EDL, Casuals United can probably best be read as one of the post-National Front splinters which uses panic about radical Islam as a gateway drug for more traditional far-right causes related to Northern Ireland, generalised racism and "commie"-bashing, and their online propaganda goes down the reliably contradictory root of trying to look terrace-tough (skinheads and C.P. Company goggle jackets) and claiming victimhood. The P&MS faction, it seemed, were dedicated to opposing "left-wing groups" who were "infiltrating" non-league football – these "left-wing groups", of course, are all, with various degrees of explicitness, represented as middle-class (once again, the fact notwithstanding that a decent portion of the vocal far-right seem to be self-employed tradesmen with earnings far in excess of the average university lecturer).

The first "success" of the P&MS came at tiny Gloucestershire club Mangotsfield United. At Mangotsfield, a small group, calling itself the "Inter-Village Firm" – a play, of course, on West Ham's Inter-City Firm – had been thriving for a few years. While not particularly militant, the group erred to the left, and had made fan friendships with similar groups in Britain and, perhaps more tellingly, in Europe. Although the IVF were in many senses a pastiche of leftist *ultraismo*, they did display some anti-racist and anti-fascist banners at grounds. Exploiting an FA directive against political imagery in football, the P&MS (and likeminded non-members) began to write letters of complaint *about a club that they had visited at best once*: the FA responded by taking action which forced Mangotsfield's board to prohibit the flags.

Encouraged by this victory over an ultras group with a membership of around twenty people, the P&MS turned their attention to Clapton and the Ultras. Fully aware that a side in the Essex Senior League could not afford policing costs, the right-wingers began an online campaign designed to suggest that they would start appearing at Clapton games and attempting to cause trouble. Acting in the understanding that they would be vastly outnumbered if they did, it was an attempt to call the Ultras' bluff by drawing them into a conflict which would, in theory, result in a forced disbandment as their ongoing presence would necessitate unaffordable policing. The right-wingers started to goad their newfound nemesis with the slogan "We go where we want", an excerpt from their adaptation of the Beach Boys' 'Sloop John B', a tune which has been put in the service of a variety of needling taunts at British football grounds in recent times. This, of course, came down once again to a question of authenticity, or the subtle implication of its opposite: the politics of reaction can go where they want because they are *real*, and they are real because they *can go where they want*. The paramilitary semiotics of fascist populism turn on this relation between self-announced bravery or indomitability and the truth of a phantasmatic *vox populi* which has, apparently, been hitherto repressed; that this in some way constitutes the representation of an opinion which is risky to hold – and therefore demands indomitable advocacy – is an ideological keystone of the contemporary far-right. When they did "go where they want", however, and attempted to harass Clapton supporters, who they had attempted to satirise on the grounds of a putatively inauthentic lack of toughness, at a game in a suburb of Southend, they were, according to most accounts of the event, met with far sterner resolve than expected. Soon, the group declared that it was no longer interested in non-league football and promised to concentrate instead on a supposed creeping politicisation of the game at higher levels. Nevertheless, their activities had alerted a wider section of the far-right to the Ultras' "ruining of football", a crime that was punished summarily with a violent ambush carried out before a pre-season friendly with Thamesmead in summer 2015.

In all of the instances described, what is repeatedly visible is the desire on the part of several species of right-wing opinion to claim popular legitimacy by making statements with varying degrees of explicitness about the political "truth" of football. In each case, the argument is that any alliance, or even juxtaposition, between progressive causes and the sport is inorganic, a gesture of politicisation which corrupts the – highly spurious, as we have seen – ontological purity of a game which allegedly does not mix with politics. Again, this is a practical demonstration of Rancière's distribution of the sensible, in which "politics" and "the political" have flexible, situationally adaptable meanings: elements of the groups who have campaigned against antifascist imagery in stadia were also involved in a campaign against UEFA when the governing body of European football said that England could not wear Remembrance Poppies on their kit in a 2011 friendly against Spain. The mutating significance of the poppy since the beginning of Britain's involvement in the War on Terror has seen it shift from being a generic symbol of *regret* about war, albeit one tinged with some patriotic relevance, to a symbol of *pride* in the UK military. Each year, Premier League clubs now display the poppy on their shirt during the games closest to 11 November, and to refuse to wear the emblem, as Sunderland's Irish midfielder James McClean did in 2012, is to invite potentially serious opprobrium. Yet the poppy, we hear, is not "political" in the way that an antifascist symbol is, because it is commemorative: to wear one is (apparently) a simple gesture of respect with no ideological protrusion, a self-contained gesture whose lack of ramifications means that it can happen simultaneously, as it were, with a comparably self-enclosing sport. Politics is inauthentic; "respect" is real and noncontaminating.

The vocabulary of authenticity in British football supporting, then, seems to turn on a metaphorics of infiltration and contamination, making it an uncanny counterpart to the logic of footballing technocracy discussed in Chapter Three. Obviously, there are colossal differences: the fantasy of technocracy seems to envisage a concluding situation of radical inauthenticity by which the virtually hermetic enclosure of the sport will be completed for the benefit of a globalised audience. By contrast, narratives of authenticity related to supporting hang on the belief that there exists a form of consuming football which turns itself against late capitalism's modern incarnation of the game without admitting an inauthentic left-wing politics. These stories – so remote from one another, yet so clearly mutually incriminating – form a couple which is itself twinned in the broader political sphere, where hypercapitalism, an unslakeable drive to enclose and consequently marketise every conceivable level of life, and atavism in several forms exist in complex entanglement.

The most visible of these forms of atavism has been discussed above, and is rarely absent from our television screens. A politics of aggrieved reaction has caught hold in Europe since the beginning of the global financial crisis: the militant patriotism encountered by the Clapton Ultras represents only a tiny fraction of a pancontinental catastrophe in the making. But there are other modes of past-fetish. Amongst the middle classes – and, once again, this is not confined to the UK – there is a fascination regarding the deep cultural origins of food, a localism which transposes the restorative nostalgia of the far-right into the palatable register of the artisanal good life. This *terroir*-worship has been theorised under various names: Alex Niven's sceptical appropriation of the term "Green Toryism" and Tom Whyman's more provocative "Cupcake Fascism" both do worthwhile work in defining retrophilia's subtly reactionary politics. More complex still, however, is the problem of the left's nostalgia for its own unattainable, and increasingly irrelevant, history, and this complexity can once again be observed in contemporary football culture and, more specifically, amongst those flying the #AMF banner.

In May 2015, the British Labour Party suffered one of their most comprehensive (and, in the context, unexpected) election defeats in modern history. Much of this was explained, problematically, in relation to three factors, namely: the mass "desertion" of left-leaning Scots to the Scottish National Party, who presented themselves as the electable choice for progressives; the effect of a failure to engage with working-class voters in England who, in many cases, either did not vote or voted for the populist right-wingers of UKIP; and, somewhat paradoxically, economic policies unappealing to the inhabitants of middle-English swing constituencies. The result was that left politics in England and Wales was faced with a decision about whether or not to persist with a Labour Party on the verge of embracing increasingly nationalistic solutions to appease those lost to UKIP and increasingly Blairite solutions to regain lost swing voters. An alternative, it seemed, was to work on the foundation of a new movement. As it stands, this contradiction has found temporary resolution with the selection of the left-winger Jeremy Corbyn as party leader, but Corbyn's position feels insecure with the ongoing prominence of mischief-making Blairites within the Parliamentary Labour Party.

Much of the intra-party briefing against Corbyn, whose elevation from the back benches was the result of an enormous grassroots recruitment of new members in the wake of electoral catastrophe, centred on the inauthenticity of his support base. This formed a continuum with what had taken place before the election. In the run-up to May, Labour found, or tried to find, a way of claiming progressive legitimacy while pushing two disturbingly reactionary lines of argument, namely their election pledge to place tough controls on immigration and their understated redefinition of their constituency from "working-class people" to "working people". They did this by mobilising their campaign teams to deploy an imagery based on squarely social-democratic successes, reminding, or attempting to remind, Britain that postwar Labour had been (largely) responsible for one of the most substantial alleviations of poverty and its effects in European history. Every billboard pledging to clamp down on immigration, then, was made to serve as a palimpsest which also, at least figuratively, displayed an image of the party singing the Internationale in a new hospital in 1945. Threatened from the left by the SNP, the Scottish Labour Party were particularly guilty of this drive to present themselves as the authentically socialist option.

However, right-Labour nostalgia selects as its authentic constituency a phantasmatic audience of mid-century industrial workers. It tells no *real* story for the students leaving university immured in debts made possible in the first instance by decisions taken by Labour, nor does it make any convincing attempt to represent the vast numbers of precarious workers who are the 21st century's true equivalent to the industrial working class exalted in 1945. Yet to point this out is to seem to break ranks with a working-class heritage that takes its place in the order of what goes without saying. Anecdotal, perhaps, but prior to the election I saw much in the way of (relatively comfortable) people from the generation above my own talking retroactively about how they were voting Labour because "that's what you do". The ongoing possibility, potentially – but only potentially – assuaged by Corbyn's leadership, that there is no space on the left, at least in England, for the current generation of people in their thirties and twenties to define their own version of political authenticity is disturbing.

A labour movement ossifiying in the triangle formed by Blairism, right-populism and postwar social democracy, and a mindset within football that relies on a highly specific, largely reactionary, model of authenticity when picturing "real" supporters possess a common cause, namely the misperception of the working class as something extant in its pre-Thatcherite form. In an era of socialised housing (or easy squatting), relatively high unemployment pay, cheap match tickets and affordable public transport, an industrial working class *could* form the body of the crowd at a football match. The decimation of these social-democratic possibilities has had the twin effect of producing, on one hand, a wholly impoverished, disenfranchised class who are economically excluded from most professional football and, on the other, an expanded petit bourgeoisie whose accession to property expanded their disposable income. Between these poles lies a group who live in differing forms of precariousness: zero-hour workers, entry-level professionals on low-paid and fixed-term contracts, renters, immigrant workers. This is a section of society who, if they can afford to go to football at all, run the risk of being marked out, somehow or other, as "inauthentic", as not properly working class according to an archaic rubric of class based on industrial, social-democratic society.

Much of the post-Blair Labour Party – and, arguably, the British centre-left in general, including much union infrastructure – and football's dominant culture bends its ear to the "hardworking people" of the lower middle classes, justifying their doing so on the basis that this is the authentic constituency of both party and sport. The questions posed by the needs of a wildly variegated precariat and a class who have, as the contemporary sociologist Imogen Tyler argues persuasively, been othered into political oblivion under neoliberalism, are beyond the range of acknowledgement of both Labour's and football's comprehension of "society". Both institutions defer constantly to the notion of authenticity despite their almost certain, if unconscious, suspicion that authenticity is now little more than a construct employed to determine horizons of political possibility. How, then, can this situation be attended to by football fans currently immobilised with frustration at the options which seem to be the only ones available to them: acquiescence to the accelerating commodification of supporting or backing an #AMF movement which seems atavistic at both of its ideological poles?

To embrace inauthenticity in football seems like a massive gamble, a roll of the dice which might well feel overly quiescent in the face of oligarch ownership, radical mediatisation, robotic refereeing, Qatari World Cups and so on. But falling back on the trope of "real" fandom seems to me just as dangerous, a path that leads to tedious one-downmanship and wheedling obscurantism. I've done it myself, and recognise the temptations, even to the point of sometimes genuinely believing that there is moral superiority in – for example – having grown up on the proverbially rain-lashed terraces of a basement-division struggler. The problem with being real, though, is that there is *always* someone realer than you are. How does a personal claim to authenticity legitimate one's political interests without threatening those of another? Are we not better served by taking flux and uncertainty as a starting point, and exploring the possibilities that arise from them?

Football as we know it came into being in such a moment of derangement and has continued to display its birth-marks, both in its rationalisation as competition and in its creation of a space in which the objectivity of rationalisation can be called into question and undermined. It therefore reproduces, or serves as an allegory for, the dialectic of capitalism, which abstracts human labour and creates both the technology and the proximity essential for liberation from this abstraction. With the future of human labour and its relationship to technology entering a stage of such all-encompassing, unforecastable ambiguity, on what grounds does it make sense for football's index of authenticity to be so grounded in vanishing social forms? Is football destined to serve as a mere reconstruction, a sporting Sealed Knot, in which we remember the industrial age, or can we, as fans, extend our horizons of expectation?

As I'm writing this final paragraph I'm also anticipating, weather allowing, going to the football tomorrow. It's a Friday evening in November and I'm sitting in my office, listening to occasional scatterings of rain on the window and reading about the 40 mile-per-hour gusts that will apparently be battering the South Coast of England at kick-off time tomorrow. Should all go to plan, I'll meet my friends in a pub around one, have a couple of drinks, recount the week gone and then head off to find the ground. At that micro-level, pretty much nothing has changed since the moment football became a sport for paying spectators, and it seems reasonable to assume that this will continue being the case, as long as people keep on *going to* matches and there's a continuation of the good work we've seen lately in terms of saying "no" to advanced forms of commercialisation. What's important, though, is that this continuity doesn't get mixed up with a manipulative narrative of authenticity, which says that we're not "real fans" if we don't pay for expensive season tickets, or merchandise, or television packages, or if we don't subscribe to restrictive notions about *who* can be a football fan and claim a stake in the game. Moreover, we have to realise, or keep on understanding, that football is only ever a microcosm of whatever exists in our broader social settings. In reality, everything we need to know about the game, bar a couple of formalities we can leave to players and referees, is beyond the touchline.

# Bibliography

Adorno, T. W. (1983). 'Notes on Kafka', in *Prisms*, trans. by Shierry Weber Nicholsen and Samuel Weber. Massachusetts: MIT Press

Barthes, R. (1972). *Mythologies*, trans. by Annette Lavers. London: Cape

---. (1992). 'The Reality Effect', *The Rustle of Language*, trans. by Richard Howard. Berkeley: University of California Press

Baudelaire, C. (2010). *The Painter of Modern Life*. London: Penguin

Beckett, S. (2008). *Endgame*. London: Faber and Faber

Benjamin, W. (1999). 'On Some Motifs in Baudelaire', in *Illuminations*, trans. by Harry Zohn. London: Pimlico

Calvin, M. (2013). *The Nowhere Men*. London: Century

Carter, A. (1991). *Wise Children*. London: Chatto & Windus

Connor, S. (2011). *A Philosophy of Sport*. London: Reaktion

Dostoyevsky, F. (2014). *Crime and Punishment*, trans. by Oliver Ready. London: Penguin

Green, H. (1929). *Living*. Darlington: J. M. Dent

Greene, G. (1938). *Brighton Rock*. London: Vintage

Hines, B. (1968). *A Kestrel for a Knave*. London: Penguin

Hornby, N. (1992). *Fever Pitch*. London: Gollancz

Johnson, B. S. (1964). *Albert Angelo*. London: Constable

---. (1969). *The Unfortunates*. London: Panther Books

---. (1973). *Christy Malry's Own Double-Entry*. London: Collins

Kafka, F. (2000). *The Castle*, trans. by J. Underwood. London: Penguin

Keane, R. (2014). *The Second Half*. London: Weidenfeld & Nicolson

Marx K. & Engels, F. (2015). *The Communist Manifesto*. London: Penguin

Niven, A. (2011). *Folk Opposition*. London: Zero

Peace, D. (2006). *The Damned United*. London: Faber and Faber

---. (2013). *Red or Dead*. London: Faber and Faber

Pound, E. (2001). 'In a Station of the Metro', in *Personae: The Shorter Poems of Ezra Pound*. London: Faber and Faber

Rancière, J. (2006). *The Politics of Aesthetics – The Distribution of the Sensible*, trans. by Gabriel Rockhill. New York; London: Continuum

Raymond, D. (2006). *He Died With His Eyes Open*. London: Serpent's Tail

Ronay, B. (2015). 'Keep off the pitch: why football makes bad art'. *Guardian*, 24 June 2015

Shackleton, L. (1955). *The Clown Prince of Soccer: His Autobiography*. London: Nicholas Kaye

Spark, M. (1960). *The Ballad of Peckham Rye*. London: Macmillan

Storey, D. (1960). *This Sporting Life*. London: Macmillan

Žižek, S. (2012). *The Year of Dreaming Dangerously*. London: Verso

## Blogs

http://splinteringboneashes.blogspot.co.uk/2010/01/negative-solidarity-and-post-fordist.html

https://infinitelyfullofhope.wordpress.com/2013/06/22/cupcakefascism/

## Acknowledgments

First of all, thanks to Alex Niven for encouraging me to write this book in the first place, and to Tariq Goddard for making me persist.

What I've written here is the outcome of extensive conversations with lots of people about football, but I'd like to express particular gratitude to my parents and step-parents, who all played formative parts in my relationship with the game, to my brother – my most longstanding and indulgent match-going companion – and to Karl Whitney and Ron Hamilton, my co-editors at Straight off the Beach. Thanks also to Robert Saunders, who gave me a conversational kick over the line towards the end. I'm also bound to offer a collective nod to everyone at Dulwich Hamlet, with special reference to those on the coach to Herne Bay that day.

I should perhaps thank my present students at the University of Gothenburg (Sussex branch) and former students at the Universities of Chichester and Brighton for putting up with extended football analogies in lectures about Lacan and Gramsci.

Two people provided invaluable critical assistance, insight and reader commentary. Robert Molloy-Vaughan and Luke Healey, respectively the best football-podcast-which-isn't-about-football co-host and the best football-focused art theorist I know, fed this park player assists worthy of Xavi and Paul Scholes.

Lastly, and profoundly, thanks to Lizzy, for all your love, encouragement and understanding.

## Repeater Books

is dedicated to the creation of a new reality. The landscape of twenty-first-century arts and letters is faded and inert, riven by fashionable cynicism, egotistical self-reference and a nostalgia for the recent past. Repeater intends to add its voice to those movements that wish to enter history and assert control over its currents, gathering together scattered and isolated voices with those who have already called for an escape from Capitalist Realism. Our desire is to publish in every sphere and genre, combining vigorous dissent and a pragmatic willingness to succeed where messianic abstraction and quiescent co-option have stalled: abstention is not an option: we are alive and we don't agree.